The Secrets To Teaching Reading

What no one ever told you

Dr. Roxie Sporleder

Teaching Basics, LLC

COPYRIGHT © 2018 by Roxie Sporleder

All Rights Reserved.

No part of this publication may be reproduced or transmitted in any form by any means, electronic or mechanical, including photocopy, recording, or any information storage and retrieval system, without permission in writing from the author.

Published by Teaching Basics, LLC
Bozeman, Montana
E-mail: roxiereading@mcn.net

Cover: Mae Verheyden

ISBN-13: 978-1-7321611-0-8

Printed in the United States of America

Also available by Dr. Roxie Sporleder:

The "Real Rules" of English, a phonics handbook
Roxie Reading Curriculums Levels 1, 2, 3, 4, and 5
Online Course on brain-based reading instruction

The Secrets to Teaching Reading

Thirty years of scientific brain research has given us amazing tools to produce proficient readers. This book identifies and integrates that research into a framework for teaching reading that is capable of producing extraordinary results. Every strategy and principle has been research validated to work in classrooms, small groups, and with individual students.

In this book you will find the secrets to success when teaching all ages, especially those who struggle with reading. It describes the skills all readers need to become proficient and the challenges of struggling readers. You will learn the secrets to teaching phonemic awareness, letter knowledge, word building, decoding, fluency, reading speed, and reading comprehension.

Resources

The "Real Rules" of English is a phoneme-based phonics handbook that gives details on all of the spellings of the sounds as well as the principles that govern them.

Roxie Reading Levels 1, 2, 3, 4 and 5 are reading curriculums designed to help students become skilled readers. These are based on ability levels and can be used in the regular classroom, with intervention groups, or with individual students.

Brain Based Literacy Instruction is a series of online interactive videos and demonstrations that explain and demonstrate the principles found in this book.

Table of Contents

The Secrets to Teaching Reading 3

Resources 4

Chapter 1: What is Possible 9
    Impact of poor reading skills 10
    There is good news! We have the tools! 11
    Meet some of my students 11
    Bring hope to the struggling reader 15

Chapter 2: Use the Right Kind of Instruction 17
    The Four Sensory Learning Styles 18
    Strengths of the kinesthetic learner 21
    What students need 24
    Special needs of Kindergarten - Grade 3 27

Chapter 3: Strategies for Kinesthetic Learners 29
    Strategies for kinesthetic learners 30
    The impact of using kinesthetic methods 34
    Re-teaching or Pre-teaching? 37

Chapter 4: The Discovery that Changes Everything! 39
    The right content and the right sequence 42
    How do poor readers read? 43
    The 4th Grade Crash 44
    Why some poor readers succeed better than others 46
    How the brain can change 47
    Skills of low-performing readers 48
    What poor readers usually DO NOT know 49
    You have the tools 50

Chapter 5: The Secret to Hearing Sounds in Spoken Words 51
    The individual sounds of speech 52
    Phoneme awareness 53
    Levels of Phonemic Awareness 53
    Voiced and unvoiced sounds 55
    Use caution in pronouncing sounds 57

Chapter 6: The Secret to Teaching Phonemic Awareness 59
    Guidelines for phonemic awareness activities 60
    Phonemic Awareness: Sound Cards 61
    Keep the game fast-paced 62
    Phonemic Awareness: Chip Game 65
    Phonemic Awareness Assessments 67

Table of Contents, cont.

Chapter 7: The Secret to Spelling Sounds..**69**
    The spellings of the speech sounds.. 70
    What you need to know about graphemes 71
    Teaching the alphabet.. 73
    Writing the letters 78
    Teaching graphemes beyond the alphabet..................................... 80

Chapter 8: The Secret of Markers: The Missing Content..............**83**
    The powerful markers: e, i, y 84
    Lesson 1: Markers make the vowel long... 84
    Lesson 2: Stopping the marker... 85
    Lesson 3: The markers make the c say /s/ 87
    Lesson 4: The markers make the g say /j/ 88
    The letter v and markers 89
    In Summary... 89

Chapter 9: The Secret to Building Words **91**
    Spelling before reading.. 92
    Guidelines for word building.. 94
    What you need to know about words... 99

Chapter 10: The Secret to Decoding Words **101**
    What is decoding? 102
    Decoding simple words.. 102
    Common decoding problems 103
    Blending the word "map"... 104
    Decoding multisyllable words.. 106
    Provide challenge words.. 108
    Pronunciation issues.. 109
    Don't underestimate students 110

Chapter 11: The Secret to Developing True Fluency......................**111**
    What is reading fluency?.. 112
    How we really read 113
    Is it a reading fluency problem? 114
    Teaching fluency 115
    In summary 117

Chapter 12: The Secret to Increasing Silent Reading Speed **119**
    Three types of silent reading.. 120
    Hindrances to silent reading speed... 121
    Activities to increase silent reading speed 122

Table of Contents, cont.

Chapter 13: The Secret of Reading at the Right Level ... **127**
- Getting students to read ... 128
- Choose the right reading level ... 130
- Provide time to read ... 133
- The classroom dilemma ... 135

Chapter 14: The Secret to Thinking about Meaning ... **137**
- What is reading comprehension? ... 138
- Accurately and fluently reading words. ... 138
- Connecting with prior knowledge ... 138
- How do we build a broad knowledge base? ... 140
- What about vocabulary? ... 140
- Strategies for building a knowledge base and vocabulary ... 142
- Connecting to what we know ... 143
- Using powerful questions to unlock meaning ... 144
- In Summary ... 148

Chapter 15: The Secret to Writing about Meaning ... **149**
- Writing about meaning ... 150
- Guidelines for all writing assignments ... 150
- The Perfect Sentence ... 152
- The question and one sentence answer ... 154
- The paragraph ... 155
- Paragraph frames ... 158
- Why is writing so important? ... 158
- In Summary ... 162

Chapter 16: Assessing Foundational Skills ... **163**
- Why do we need to assess? ... 164
- The Framework for Teaching Reading ... 165
- Four basic assessments ... 167
- What You Need To Know About A Student ... 168
- The Letter Recognition Test ... 169
- The Developmental Spelling Test ... 170
- Phonemic Awareness Assessments ... 178
- Phoneme Segmentation Assessment ... 179
- Phonemic Manipulation Assessment ... 181
- Sound Card Assessment ... 182
- Informal Reading Analysis ... 185
- Oral Reading Fluency Rubric ... 186
- Informal Reading Analysis Summary ... 187
- Ongoing formative assessment ... 188

Table of Contents, cont.

Chapter 17: Special Situations **189**
    English Language Learners 190
    Hearing impaired 191
    Vision impairments 192
    Intellectual disability 195
    In Summary 196

Chapter 18: The Plan **197**
    What you need to do 198
    A special note on cross-lateral exercise 201
    You have the tools 201

Appendix A: The Graphemes for the Speech Sounds **203**

Appendix B: Actions for the Sounds **207**

Appendix C: The "Real Rules" of English **215**

Appendix D: Answers **221**

Bibliography **224**

Index **232**

Chapter 1:
What is Possible

**Every individual has the potential
to become a skilled reader.
It is never too late.**

Impact of poor reading skills

Reading is a gateway skill for all other learning. In fact, it is a gateway skill for a productive life. If an individual can learn how to read well, the possibilities become endless. But if that individual cannot read well, hope diminishes and the future seems bleak.

Experience of the poor reader

Poor readers bear the heavy burden of failure. "I can't." "I'm stupid." I've heard those statements countless times. They see others that can read, but they can't. Their conclusion is that there must be something terribly wrong with them.

They usually hate school and often hate themselves. Every day they are asked to perform tasks that are impossible for them to do. They may withdraw, or they may become aggressive. Low self-esteem is generalized to every area of life. The anxiety may lead to depression or juvenile delinquency and drugs. If they are not supported at home, they may drop out of school, glad to leave a place that tore away at their soul.

These students are often tested again and again, labeled, and placed in special groups, special programs, and sometimes even in special classrooms. They may be called dyslexic, learning disabled, writing disabled, ADD, or ADHD. But some are *not* test and labeled. These students struggle on their own with little extra help.

Impact on teachers

Dedicated and caring teachers work hard to help these students. They reteach lessons but become discouraged when there is minimal change in reading skills. Many teachers feel frustrated and sad. They often just accept the fact that many struggling readers will not be able to read at grade level. They support these students as best as possible with strategies that focus on meaning and reading comprehension.

Impact on parents

Parents are shocked to find that their bright, energetic child is not doing well in school. Distraught, they look for answers but often find none. It is confusing to them that their child who is so intelligent cannot learn to read well. And no one seems to have an answer.

The impact on society

The toll on our society is devastating. The impact of poor literacy ripples through every segment of our culture and costs billions of dollars a year. Our economy, our health care system, and our criminal justice system are impacted by low reading achievement. Individuals who cannot read well are at risk for crime, mental health issues, unemployment, and poverty. The relationship to crime is so well-documented that many states determine the number of prison cells needed based on 4th grade reading scores. There is no argument that low literacy rates have a negative impact on an entire society.

There is good news! We have the tools!

Over thirty years of scientific research has provided enough information so we truly have the tools to teach students of all ages how to become proficient readers. In this book, we will look at that research, build the knowledge base to implement the research, and explore strategies that have been proven to produce skilled readers. These methods have been researched, formally tested, and demonstrated to help all students in kindergarten through 12th grade read proficiently unless they have some type of severe disability. Even those improve beyond expected levels.

An example

I worked with a group of teachers who were learning how to teach struggling readers. They mistakenly chose to teach children in special education classrooms, the most challenging type of student to teach. These were children who were never expected to read well. The teachers were amazed at the results. Their conclusion: "Every child can learn to read well." What did they do? These teachers taught the right content in the right sequence with the right instruction.

Meet some of my students[1]

Here are the stories of some of my students who went from struggling reader to skilled reader. These students were taught using a special curriculum

---

1 The names of all students in this book have been changed to protect their identity. All of these students were assessed with standardized, nationally recognized tests. Most were assessed with the *Woodcock Reading Mastery Test-R before* instruction began and at the *conclusion* of instruction.

that teaches the right content in the right sequence with the right kind of instruction. It consists of 45 *one-hour* lessons. With this curriculum, significant change is usually observed by parents and teachers within the first six to eight lessons. In addition to the one-hour lesson, students read 30 minutes a day in a book of their choice. These students were like most other struggling readers.

- They all read below grade level. Some read several grades below grade level.
- They had received various kinds of interventions without much change in their reading.
- They hated to read.
- They struggled with school. Most hated it.
- Most had low self-esteem. They considered themselves failures.

Manuel

When Manuel entered second grade, he was reading well below grade level. At the end of second grade, he still had not caught up even though many different interventions were used. Nothing seemed to work. He had made some progress, but not enough. The same pattern followed Manuel through third grade, and upon entering fourth grade, his reading level was still well below grade level. His teacher then began teaching the right content in the right sequence with the right instruction. By the end of fourth grade, Manuel was reading *above* grade level.

April

April was in second grade, but could only read a handful of words. This hindered her ability to complete the normal tasks that were required in her classroom. She was very intelligent but her lack of ability to read stumped everyone.

When I began teaching April, she caught on so quickly that I taught her two lessons per session rather than the usual one. Due to circumstances, we only completed 15 of the 45 lessons. But even with so few lessons, she gained an understanding of how the "language worked."

When she took her standardized achievement tests near the end of second grade, she scored in the 99th percentile in almost every subject—science, social studies, reading, and math. That means 99% of the students in the nation taking that test scored *below* her. She had learned to read well and now was working up to her amazing capability.

Sean

Sean was a sixth grade student who could not read a first grade primer. He had no idea how to "sound out" the simplest words and could only read words such as *it, and, I,* and *the*. Although he could not read, he loved to learn and so listened to historical fiction and other books on tape. This gave him an amazing knowledge base and vocabulary which became a definite asset when he finally did learn to read. By the end of the 45 lessons, Sean was stashing books under the seat of the van so he could squeeze in reading in any spare moment. At the beginning, he could not sound out a word or read a first grade reader and now *The Lord of the Rings* and other young adult fiction books were his favorite books.

Jakob

Jakob was a 6th grade special education student who spent most of his time in the special education room except for joining the regular classroom for Social Studies and Science. When I tested him in reading using the *Woodcock Reading Mastery Test,* a reliable and valid individual test in reading, he scored in the 0.1 percentile in all areas – Word Identification, Word Attack Skills, Passage Comprehension, Total Basic Skills, and Total Reading Skills. That means 99.9% of the students his age in the nation scored *above* him. He could not even read a first grade primer since he knew only a handful of words.

After 45 hours of instruction, Jakob could read at a beginning 4th grade level. The second year, he went through the 45 lessons again at a higher reading level and was reading at grade level. Jakob, the special education student who could only read about eight words in 6th grade, graduated from high school with his class and went on to college.

Jared

Jared was a junior in high school. His skills were higher than most struggling readers with whom I have worked, reading at a beginning 4th grade level although his ability to read unknown words was at beginning 2nd grade level. As you can imagine, school was an immense struggle for him. Once Jared realized it was possible for him to learn to read, he committed himself to the task. By the end of the 45 lessons, his reading scores were at grade level, an increase of *seven* grade levels. The most amazing part of his story is that he went on to college, maintained a grade point average above 3.0, and graduated with a degree in journalism. Today he is a avid reader and prolific writer.

John

John is a good example of a bright student who couldn't read and whose life goals changed once he became a proficient reader. When I first met him, he attended a small private school that catered to students with learning difficulties. Although he was classified as a junior in high school, he was struggling with 4th grade work in all subjects. Reading was difficult for him, and he could not spell even the simplest words. Probably the most notable characteristic of John was his persistent vocalizing "I can't." Whatever he was asked to do, his immediate response was "I can't." And most likely, he couldn't.

At the end of 45 hours of instruction spread over six months, John was reading at a 9th grade level rather than the 3rd grade level, a gain of *six* grade levels. When he realized he could read, he changed his career goal from massage therapist to lawyer. However, he had a problem. He had essentially lost all of his years of schooling because he was unable to read.

In the fall of his senior year, he called me, asking what he should do since he wanted to go to college. I suggested he go to the local university and enroll in a program that would support him in acquiring a high school equivalency diploma. They would identify areas of weakness and provide classes to prepare for the test.

Three weeks later he called me. "You'll never guess. They tested me and said that in reading and language arts I have no weaknesses. I am reading at a post-college level." Because John had learned the necessary skills, he had continued to grow in his reading, something I have observed with many other students. Within three months after completing my reading program, he was reading at a post-college level and preparing to go to college to become a lawyer.

Teach the right content in the right sequence
with the right kind of instruction.

None of these students could learn to read with the methods currently used in most classrooms across the nation. But they were successful when the principles of reading found in scientific research were implemented. We will show you how.

Bring hope to the struggling reader

Struggling readers are devastated by their inability to read. They have given up hope and have resigned themselves to being a failure because they feel there is something tragically wrong with them. You are the one who can make the difference in their lives. In my own experience with students of all ranges of abilities, disabilities, and ages, I have found the research is correct. It produces results beyond anything we expected. Students can learn to read well.

You can make a difference.

To make a difference, you must believe these students can achieve, never giving up hope on any of them. Your beliefs about them will influence your behavior and ultimately their achievement. Well-known research by psychologists have proven that teachers' beliefs about their students make a difference. When teachers mistakenly think the low ability students in their classroom are in the high-ability group, they are more patient and provide more explanations. These low-ability students often rise to meet the expectations of the teachers, performing more like high-ability students. It is the belief of the teacher that has made the difference.

Your beliefs about the abilities of your students will profoundly influence their achievement.

When we assume students have little hope of improvement if they have not learned to read at grade level by the end of third grade, we doom them to social, psychological, physical, and financial suffering. I have worked with many high school students who could only read a beginning primer, but ended up reading above grade level.

Applying the principles of the research found in this book can make the difference. It takes some students longer to learn and some need more practice. But they learn. Others just need the right kind of instruction to make it all click.

All students can learn the next thing
to hat they already know.

IMPORTANT DEFINITIONS

Read through the following definitions. They define the labels that many poor readers receive.

Dyslexia	Difficulties learning to read. This includes difficulty with word recognition, spelling, and decoding. This results in poor reading comprehension and slow growth in vocabulary and background knowledge. It is not related to intelligence. It does not necessarily mean students will write letters backwards. Many students do this until age seven or eight even if they are not dyslexic.
Learning Disability	Difficulties learning knowledge and skills at the level expected for their age. This disability is not associated with a physical handicap.
Writing Disabled	Difficulties with spelling and putting ideas into language in an organized way. Their handwriting tends to be messy.
ADD Attention Deficit Disorder	Difficulties learning due to the inability to think about or pay attention to things for very long.
ADHD Attention Deficit and Hyperactivity Disorde)	Difficulties staying focused and paying attention like ADD but also has difficulty controlling behavior and hyperactivity

Chapter 2:
Use the Right Kind of Instruction

**Everybody is a genius.
But if you judge a fish by its ability
to climb a tree,
it will live its whole life believing
it is stupid.**

-- Albert Einstein

How we learn

Why do some students learn to read quite easily, and others fail to become proficient readers? Many students struggle to learn to read even though they have average or above average intelligence. Some of them are the most brilliant, creative people I have ever met. About 95% of poor readers fall into this category.

Understanding the four sensory learning styles will help us answer this question. These learning styles are the ways we process, understand, and remember information. We use all of these styles but usually one or two of these styles help us more than the others. As you read the following descriptions, try to determine what your sensory learning style might be. Also think about how learning styles might affect learning to read.

The Four Sensory Learning Styles

	Body	In order to Learn	Supportive Activities
Visual	eyes	I must **read** it to understand it.	reading watching
Auditory	ears	I must **hear** it or talk about it to understand it.	listening and talking
Tactile	small muscles (hands)	I must **write** it to understand it.	writing drawing
Kinesthetic	large muscles (arms, legs, body)	I must **do** something to understand it.	writing at whiteboard, use of manipulatives, demonstrations, experiments, acting out, moving about the classroom

Visual Learner - I must read it to understand it.

We all know this kind of person. Maybe you are one of them. These individuals can hear an explanation, listen to instructions, or be shown how to do something but have difficulty processing information unless they can read it themselves. They need written instructions, a textbook, or a written list.

My daughter says, "Listen to this paragraph. What do you think about it?"

I'm not much help unless I can read the paragraph. It is as if my mind can't hold those spoken words long enough to process them and make a judgment. In lecture classes, these students *must* take notes in order to have some kind of written record to read later. These individuals usually do well in school because it centers around written information. They are often independent learners because they do not need to hear explanations or be shown how to complete a task. They can read and understand.

Auditory Learner - I must hear it to understand it.

These individuals can read information, but not understand it well unless there is a discussion or a lecture. If there is no auditory explanation of some kind, they may resort to talking to themselves. In college, they dare not miss a lecture class because they would be left to trying to understand the information from the textbook on their own. Small discussion groups of various types support this kind of learner.

This learning style is so weak for me that if I were forced to learn only by listening and not allowed to read, take notes, or try to practice it, I would fail. It would be impossible for me to succeed.

Tactile Learner – I must write it to understand it.

These learners must take notes of some kind in order to process information. It might be a formal outline or random words on a page that look like doodling. When these individuals listen to a lecture, sit in a meeting, or read a book, they write. An interesting fact about these learners is that they may never read what they have written. The process of writing is what brings understanding, not reading it afterwards.

Sometimes a lecturer will say, "Just listen. Don't take notes." That is death to understanding for this type of learner. They *must* write in order to learn. However, it is just the opposite for an auditory learner. If they are *required* to take notes in class, it can significantly interfere with their learning.

Tactile learners also benefit from any activity that requires the use of the fine muscles such as picking up or touching objects. Manipulating cards or objects that require both fine and large muscles benefit both tactile and kinesthetic learners.

Kinesthetic Learner – I must do something to understand it.

These individuals, if they are strongly kinesthetic, do not learn well by reading, listening, or taking notes. Think about it. This is what school is all about. How do they learn then?

They must engage in activities that require the use of the large muscles. **They must move in order to learn.** In the classroom, this includes any activity that uses the full arm, such as writing at a whiteboard, manipulating flash cards, handling game components, or using a computer. Obviously, demonstrations, experiments, acting, or activities that require movement from one area of the classroom to the other also support this type of learner.

Pictures that represent actions also help these students remember information. A kinesthetic learner told me that when he takes notes, he also draws a picture. When he looks at the picture later, he can recall what the teacher said almost word for word.

It is interesting that visual diagrams also aid these individuals in understanding. It organizes the information for them, something the centers in the left side of the brain usually do for other types of learners. It also provides an overview of the entire idea, something that is important for this type of learner.

These are the students that are forgotten and left behind in the classroom. Traditional classrooms focus on reading, listening, and writing, but these students do not learn well with those learning methods. These learners are often brilliant, and if not discouraged, go on to do great things. But many times they become defeated, ashamed, and even drop out of school. Society loses the significant intellectual contributions these individuals could have made.

In many cases, students who struggle with reading are kinesthetic learners. That means we must include kinesthetic methods when we teach reading and not just focus on the visual, auditory, and tactile. That is why special attention is given to this particular learning style for every activity in this book.

Poor readers are often kinesthetic learners.

Strengths of the kinesthetic learner

What are the strengths of kinesthetic learners? These individuals are some of the most brilliant in our society, but the way they process information differs from the rest of the world. And because of that, many are labeled with dyslexia or learning disabilities. What are these learners like?

1. **They usually like art, music, athletics, computers, mechanics, and/or science.**

   These individuals are creative and imaginative. They often think "outside of the box." They enjoy working with their hands. You will often see them drawing or doodling during class.

   By the time, they get to high school, we have unintentionally "sorted" the kinesthetic learners into a program all of their own, usually leaving them out of college prep courses.

Visual, Auditory, Tactile Learners	Kinesthetic Learners
English	Technology Ed
Math	Music
Science	Visual Arts
History	Drama
	Industrial Arts

   In the early 1990's when computers were not common in schools, a small rural school brought in computers for a week to introduce both teachers and students to basic functions. In that same school, six 5th grade students spent most of their time in the Resource Room, struggling with every aspect of school.

   However, that week was different. Who went from room to room, teaching both teachers and students how to use the computers? It was these six 5th grade students from the Resource Room. They "got it" easily when most of the others didn't.

2. **They usually think in pictures not words.**

   They usually process the world about them in pictures and not in words. This is an asset when you are an architect, artist, mechanic, or other individual in the creative arts. To perform well, they must be able to visualize the whole as if it were completed.

Another aspect of thinking in pictures is the depth and breadth of ideas communicated through a picture.

> "A picture thinker can think a single picture of a concept that might require hundreds or thousands of words to describe. Einstein's theory of relativity came to him in a daydream in which he traveled beside a beam of light. His vision lasted only seconds, yet spawned scores of textbooks to explain it."
>
> --Davis, *The Gift of Dyslexia*, p. 100

This is why seeing or drawing pictures are such powerful ways for these types of learners to understand and remember information.

3. **They are curious and need to know why.**

   They are usually "out of the box" thinkers. They want to know *why* things are like they are. Many students just want to know "how" to do things. That is not how kinesthetic individuals look at the world. "Why" is more important than "how." Teachers may mistake their asking "why" as a sign of disrespect or trying to get out of work, but there is a genuine need for them to know "why." That ability is what makes some of them amazing inventors, scientists, and entrepreneurs.

4. **They usually think in three-dimensions.**

   Unless you are kinesthetic, it is difficult to grasp visualizing everything in three dimensions. One scientist with whom I talked, said, "I see the x, y, z axis in mathematics in three-dimensions. I can turn it around in my head in any direction."

   Flat two - dimensions   **Three - dimensions**

   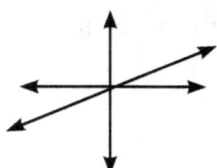 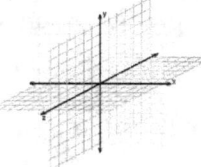

   Imagine, then, going to school and having to read and write in a two-dimensional world. How do you place the letter *b* on paper? In your head you can turn it in any direction, even upside down, but what is the correct direction on a two-dimensional piece of paper? It does not come naturally. You will need cues to remind you how to do it until it becomes automatic. This is why some of these learners have a tendency to write some of the letters backwards.

Sometimes kinesthetic learners say they do not see three-dimensionally, but if you press them about the pictures in their mind, they concede they are three-dimensional.

5. **They often need to see the big picture.**

   Many kinesthetic learners find it difficult to take bits and pieces of information and put it together to make sense. Many process new and difficult information globally. If they see the big picture, then they are able to place the details in the proper place. Graphic organizers and graphic overviews help these learners see the whole all at once. There are hundreds of variations of graphic organizers that can be found on the internet. Here are some examples that help students see the "big picture."

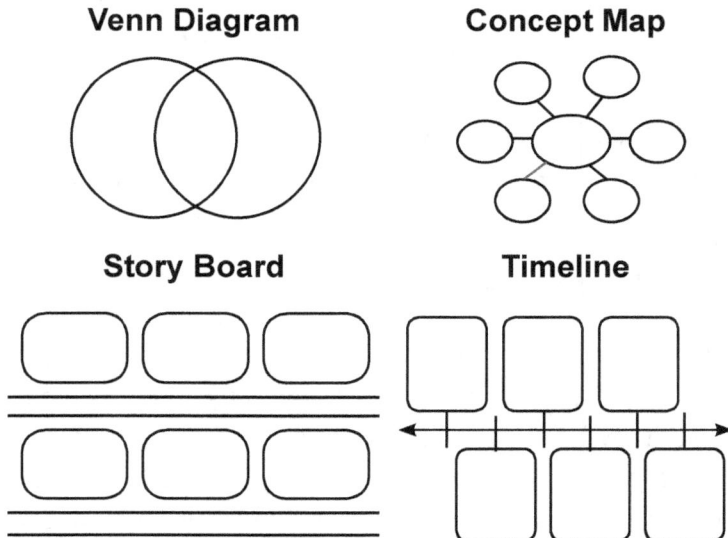

6. **They are often highly intelligent.**

   Their lack of ability to function in a traditional classroom has nothing to do with intelligence. In fact, some of the most brilliant people are kinesthetic. Many of our famous scientists, mathematicians, entrepreneurs, musicians, and actors are kinesthetic learners.

7. **They have to move in order to learn.**

    They must use their large muscles in order to process information. If movement is not a planned part of learning, they may tap their pencils, shift their legs, or get out of their seats. What strategies need to be incorporated into our teaching to support this type of learner? We must know how to meet the needs of the kinesthetic learner if they are to be successful in the classroom.

> "Many children seen at the National Reading Diagnostics Institute have a diagnosis of Attention Deficit Hyperactivity Disorder (ADHD). Yet in-depth reading evaluations of these youngsters often reveal that rather than having an attention disorder, they are *simply kinesthetic learners*. They need to engage in gross motor (large-muscle) activity to learn best. Once they are given the opportunity to learn through the proper methods, their ADHD-like behavior often disappears."
>
> --Ricki Linksman
> *The Fine Line Between ADHD and Kinesthetic Learners.*

What strategies need to be incorporated into our teaching to support this type of learner? We must know how to meet the needs of the kinesthetic learner if they are to be successful in the classroom.

What students need

One of the most important needs we have is the need for a sense of achievement. When it comes to reading, many students have failed so many times they have internalized failure and feel they themselves are a mistake. It becomes their identity. They don't expect to succeed at anything. We hear the words, "I can't" or "I'm dumb." The stress of failure snowballs into more stress and failure. Students may quit trying and even hate school.

Few people will attempt to perform a task for which they believe they have little opportunity for success.

But we can turn that around. Besides using all four learning styles in our teaching, here are some other ways we can help students gain a sense of achievement as they engage in reading and writing activities.

1. **Begin every lesson with what they already know.**

    Begin with content students know and can do. Then gradually increase the difficulty. For example, if they know two letters of the alphabet, start with activities using those two letters. Then add *one* more letter. *Students should never be working with multiple concepts they do not know.*

2. **Warn students when the activity will get more difficult.**

    After students have been successful in working with concepts they know, tell them when you are going to introduce something new. Let them know you are going to help them learn the new concept. The practice of warning seems to help students to mentally "rise to the challenge." They know it is something that is more difficult and may require some help from you. It is not a sign of failure if they can't do it. Help them so they succeed, and then commend them for getting it right.

3. **Use the principle of errorless learning.**

    The basic principle of errorless learning is to anticipate and prevent errors so students complete the activity correctly as they learn new concepts. *Give students all the help they need to perform a task without error.* Give clues and ask questions that guide them to the correct answer. This is in contrast to the traditional approach where students complete the activity with mistakes and later receive feedback on any errors.

    - "Write the word *like*. Listen carefully to the sounds.
    - What do you hear at the end? How do you spell it? What is making the l say /ī/? **Tell them if they don't know.**
    - **Students write the word like.**
    - "Now change the word *like* to *likely*.
    - What do you hear at the end of the word *likely*? How do you spell it?" **Tell them if they don't know.**
    - "We just add it right onto the word." **Students write the word likely.**

Errorless learning reduces anxiety and discouragement and provides students with a positive sense of achievement. When you use errorless learning, students not only accomplish more than we or they thought they could, but they also begin to grow in their confidence. They actually produce work that is correct for a change.

4. **Provide immediate feedback.**

   When you provide immediate feedback as part of the instruction, students are able to correct any errors immediately. The final product is free of errors. This solidifies the correct answers and accelerates learning.

5. **Teach concepts at the instructional level of students.**

   Teach at a level where students *need* some help in the form of clues and questions in order to be successful. This establishes a comfortable, safe environment for learning. ***It is also the level where students make the most progress.*** If students only work on activities where they are expected to perform independently, they will not make as much progress. Students should never work at the frustration level where the task is too difficult for them even if you give them some help.

What I can do   What I can do with   What I can do with
independently   a little help   some help

6. **Provide instruction that ensures success**

   Building success into the lives of students relieves stress and starts the spiral upward. Little successes build on little successes and grow into a sense of achievement. Success is motivating. Students who disliked reading and writing now enjoy it because they can actually perform successfully. I think of my students Jared who ended up getting a college degree in journalism of all things, Sean who stashed books under the van seat so he could snatch a little reading time, and John who chose being a lawyer (just think of the reading) as his career goal. These were students who hated reading, despised themselves for their failures, and counted on doing not much with their lives.

   People want to learn everything unless they become discouraged.

Special needs of Kindergarten - Grade 3

There are additional considerations for students in kindergarten through third grade. These children are limited in what they can do merely because of their physical and mental development. Don't expect more than what they can do.

Attention spans are short.

An attention span is the length of time a child can remain engaged in one activity. Whoever did the research on attention spans did it right. These are invariably true, and the price for not following them is behavioral problems. It is almost impossible for children to stay attentive once the time limit has expired. However, once you change the activity or the place, you can begin a new time span.

In observing elementary classrooms, I noted that one minute past the attention span, one student was off-task. Within five minutes past the attention span, several students were off-task. Teachers can lose control of a learning activity merely because students are expected to work beyond their attention span.

Attention Spans	
Kindergarten	5 - 10 minutes
Grades 1 - 3	15 - 20 minutes

Despite these guidelines some children will engage in an activity that is highly interesting to them for longer periods of time. However, when you plan your lessons, pay strict attention to the attention spans.

Their fine muscles are not developed.

The fine muscles necessary for coloring, writing, and cutting are not fully developed until age nine. That means many of these children will not have good control over the pencil, crayon, or scissors. As they grow, these muscles will develop and you will see improvement.

When children's fine motor skills are not fully developed:
- It may be difficult for them to color within the lines.
- It may be difficult for them to cut on the lines.

- Their letters may be large or slightly malformed.
- They can only write for a very short amount of time before their hand gets "tired."
- They will shake their hand after writing for a short time, or just be off task.

Be aware of these limitations.
- Don't expect children to write letters and words perfectly.
- Don't expect children to write for long periods of time.

Five to fifteen minutes of writing is usually maximum for children five to eight years old. ***Alternate writing and cutting tasks with reading or listening.***

When planning activities for these children, alternate between tasks that require fine muscles and those that do not. Here is an example of how to alternate tasks that require fine muscles with tasks that require large muscles.

Large muscles	Fine muscles of the eye	Large muscles	Fine muscles of the hand
act out the sound	read	Phonemic awareness games	write

Also, be aware of the differences in fine muscle development among children. A second grade student may have poor penmanship while some five-year-olds seem to have very good penmanship. It all depends on the fine muscle development of each child.

In Summary

1. Use all four sensory learning styles: visual, auditory, tactile, and kinesthetic.
2. Make an extra effort to include kinesthetic activities.
3. Use errorless learning and immediate feedback. Teach at the instructional level.
4. For K - 3, alternate fine muscle activities with large muscle activities.
5. For K - 3, pay strict attention to the limits of attention spans.

Chapter 3: Strategies for Kinesthetic Learners

Kinesthetic learners are "hands-on learners" who actually concentrate better when movement is involved.

Strategies for kinesthetic learners

What do kinesthetic learners need in the classroom to learn? Reading is usually taught using the visual, auditory, and tactile sensory learning styles. The teacher writes, explains, and shows flash cards. Students read texts and fill out worksheets. The kinesthetic learner is usually forgotten when teachers choose activities. To prevent squandering the intellectual capital of these students, we must design instruction that meets their learning needs. If we incorporate kinesthetic strategies into the teaching of reading and writing, these students can excel.

- **Whiteboards**

    Whiteboards, chalkboards, and easels all require the use of the full arm because markers and chalk require more movement than a pencil or pen. Even more large muscle movement is required if students stand at a board or easel. Every classroom should at minimum have individual whiteboards that students can use on a daily basis. Students can use them to do their own work, respond to answers asked by the teacher, or to make a "whiteboard" copy of what the teacher is writing for the class such as how to solve a math problem.

    A kinesthetic learner often finds it easy to spell and solve problems at a whiteboard but difficult to do the same work with pencil and paper. A high school student said to me, "I can't do these physics problems on paper for some reason. I just can't understand what to do. But when I do them at the chalkboard, they are easy. I always do my work there first and then just copy it onto my paper."

    If you go into the graduate student offices in almost any university mathematics department, you will find them lined with chalkboards or whiteboards.

    The whiteboard is a kinesthetic learner's best friend.

    Can iPads be used? Yes. Always check to see if the apps you use require full arm movement and not just the movement of the fingers as in writing with pencil and paper. Also make sure students can easily erase and correct their work.

- **Flashcards, activity cards, 3x5 cards**

    Manipulating any type of card requires the use of the full arm. Unfortunately in the traditional classroom, the teacher is the one who handles the flashcards. One parent asked me how to help her son learn his multiplication tables. She was frustrated because for months she had used flashcards with him, and he still didn't know them. I asked, "Who is manipulating the flash cards?" She was. She went home and had her son handle the cards. She came back in two weeks and said he knew all of his multiplication tables.

Students, not the teacher, need to manipulate the cards.

Activity cards can be designed for all types of topics. My students had individual cards for math facts, geometry concepts, the parts of speech, the parts of a sentence, the spellings of the sounds of our language, and responses for test review. Students used these for individual review or for responses to questions asked to the class or group.

I had a third grade student who could barely do any work with pencil and paper. Her kindergarten teacher had assumed she was intellectually disabled and had sent home a brochure titled *"How to Help Your Mentally Retarded Child."* But she wasn't. Accommodations had to be made for her because she could complete only three or four items out of fifteen or twenty on any worksheet. But she could slap down the correct response cards faster than anyone in the class. She was sharp but just couldn't function well with traditional classroom materials.

Older students who have difficulty remembering important material can place that information on 3 x 5 cards (and maybe include a drawing). Manipulating the cards helps them place that information into memory.

- **Manipulatives**

    Manipulatives are objects such as counting chips, letter tiles, blocks, and shapes. Students use these to solve problems and respond to teacher prompts rather than giving an oral or written reply. Without these, kinesthetic learners usually "follow the crowd" with oral replies, mimicking what everyone else is doing without true understanding. If the response is to be written on paper, they struggle.

- **Demonstrations and experiments**

  Demonstratons and experiments are three-dimensional experiences that help kinesthetic learners remember concepts. It is best if these learners perform these themselves or at the least assist someone else. Participating in the demonstration meets the additional need for large muscle movement in order to understand and remember. You will find that these types of learners will often volunteer to participate, anxious for a way to get out of their seats.

- **Computers**

  Kinesthetic learners usually excel at understanding and using computers, something that is challenging for others. Have you ever heard people ask, "*Why* is this computer...?" Kinesthetic learners love to learn "why."

  Also, the touch screen, joy sticks, and mouse all require large muscle movement. Straight keyboarding is tactile and is usually more difficult for many of these types of learners.

- **Small group activities**

  Small group activities usually require movement within the classroom, at least before and after the group. In addition, many activities give the kinesthetic learner more freedom to move during the group. If a small group activity requires evaluation or problem solving, this meets their need to discover "why" and think "outside of the box."

- **Dramatization**

  Any kind of acting meets three needs of the kinesthetic learner. It is a three-dimensional experience that imprints a picture in the memory, requires the use of the large muscles, and is creative and imaginative. Learners can act out sounds, vocabulary words, stories, historical events, and the way blood moves through the body. Be creative in the way you incorporate drama.

- **Games**

  Almost all games require some kind of large muscle movement whether they be board games or playground games. I know many kinesthetic learners who make up their own games to meet their need for problem solving and creativity.

- **Diagrams and graphic organizers**

    Simple diagrams and graphic organizers present information at a glance. Concepts are organized to show relationships in a few words. It meets the need of the kinesthetic learner to see the "big picture." It is best if these learners can design and draw these themselves.

- **Pictures and drawings**

    A picture is "worth a thousand words" and that is why they are so helpful to the kinesthetic learner. For any concept, find pictures that illustrate it. These learners may also enhance their notes with drawings for the same reason. When I read stories aloud to the class, I allowed students to write or draw if they wished. They did not have to just sit and listen.

- **Problem-solving and evaluating**

    These learners ask "why" and not "how" even though many times they *should* be asking "how." Problem-solving activities challenge them to learn. Set up learning situations where they can analyze and evaluate problems. The "problem of the week," the discovery of patterns within sentences or geometric shapes, and the use of "why" questions in any subject are examples of effective strategies.

- **Creative projects**

    Creative projects provide great opportunities for movement, creativeness, asking "why," and expressing concepts as a "big picture."

- **Real objects, field trips, and simulations**

    These require large muscle movement, bring concepts to life, and are the ultimate in "big picture" representations.

Many of these methods are not traditionally used in school, let alone in teaching reading. That is why students who depend on the kinesthetic learning style find school "isn't for them," or worse yet, damages their view of themselves. Look at everything you teach and begin incorporating these strategies into every concept. In the following chapters, we will show you how to use them to teach reading.

In the early 1900's, Dr. Grace Fernald, a researcher and professor at the University of California, successfully helped thousands of students learn how to read at grade level using kinesthetic methods. She did not have the advantage of the current brain research, but she understood the needs of these learners.

> "It seems that most cases of reading disability are due to *blocking of the learning process* by use of limited, uniform methods of teaching. These methods, although they have been used successfully with the majority of children, make it impossible for certain children to learn. . .
>
> "We do not claim that all cases of reading disability are due to the use of methods that *omit kinesthetic* factors, but merely that such cases exist and that under our present system of education, a large percentage of the cases of extreme disability are due to the above ."
>
> --Grace M. Fernald, 1943

The impact of using kinesthetic methods

The following is a true story of my work with Drew, a third grade student who struggled with learning. The first time I met Drew was in the Resource Room late in September. He was in 3rd grade and spent two hours in the morning working on language skills.

****

Drew comes into the room to work. He has a sad and sullen expression on his face.

"I can't read. I'm dumb," he seriously announces to me as we begin work.

I point out the story that he read to me perfectly the day before. It does not convince him.

"Would you like to write on the chalkboard?" I ask. His eyes lighten and he gives a nod. I suggest he write a sentence on the chalkboard, we would fix it together, and then he could write it on a large sheet of construction paper and draw a picture to go with it. His serious expression returns. "I can't spell. I'm dumb. I can't write anything."

I could see that he had made up his mind that the task was impossible. "You can work on the computer for awhile, and then we can think about a sentence when you come back."

Drew loves working on the computer and without any hesitation, he selects a program and stays at the computer for almost twenty minutes. You could see he felt good about himself when he returned to the chalkboard area.

We discuss some of the things he could write about and the way he could say it. I am very reassuring and supportive in my tone of voice and in my words. Suddenly he has an idea. He writes on the chalkboard: "Thir is a mnster undr mi bed."

"I can read your sentence, Drew. I know exactly what you wrote!" I am smiling. He grins. I read it to him.

"That is a very good sentence, Drew. Should we fix it so you can write it on the paper and draw a picture?" He nods, very pleased with himself.

We go through the sentence word by word, discussing every thing that is right and discussing what can be changed. He makes the corrections with very little help. He grins. He has felt tremendous achievement.

I get the construction paper out for him and his sullen expression returns. "I can't draw. I'm dumb."

He carefully writes his sentence. Then he makes a few marks on the paper under his sentence.

"It looks like a very scary monster to me! I like it!" He colors his picture although he is still looking as if he is unsure. However, he is pleased enough to find a place to display his work when it is finished.

The next morning, Drew comes into the resource room and the first thing he says is, "Can I write another sentence on the board?"

"Wonderful! Yes, you may!"

Without any hesitation he writes: "I wnt on a vakasun." I feel very pleased that he has enough courage to take the risk to write.

"May I read it to you?" I ask.

He grins and nods. I read it to him. We fix the sentence, discussing every right word and figuring out how to fix the mistakes. I commend him for not being afraid of using *vacation* even though it is a long word. He is happy. He has experienced many successes in one sentence. Drew draws another wonderful picture under his sentence. He displays this picture, too, looking as if the sense of achievement has totally changed his outlook on reading and writing.

That was my last day in the Resource Room. I wish I could teach Drew every day. He is extremely capable. Two weeks later I see Drew come into his regular 3rd grade classroom. He had been gone all morning to the Resource Room. He comes into the room in the afternoon. Defeat is in his eyes. He is angry. He refuses to do any work at all for the rest of the day. "I can't. I'm not smart. I can't read."

The assigned classroom work gives Drew no opportunity for success, and he has come from two hours of school work with no evidence of achievement. It is at least 80% failure.

* * * * * * *

This story was documented as it happened. This child was intelligent, but could not read and write. He had already internalized failure. However, when given the opportunity to engage in kinesthetic activities, he did so. Working at the computer, writing on the chalkboard while he was standing, and drawing a picture to go with his sentence were activities he could complete. Notice how he didn't mind correcting his work when he knew the final product would be perfect. Which it was. The principles of errorless learning and immediate feedback supported his learning.

Notice how just a tiny bit of achievement quickly turned his attitude. *In just one day*, he was willing to write and read, knowing that in the end there would be success. In order to exist with any kind of emotional health, we need at least 80% success in what we do. The work he found in his 3rd grade classroom was all visual, auditory, and tactile, and at this point, above his instructional level. There was no opportunity for success in what he was learning or in how he was learning it.

Although, kinesthetic learners comprise the largest percentage of individuals who cannot read proficiently, students with hearing and speech impairments, cognitive delays, or just learning English also have difficulty learning to read. Most of these also benefit from instruction that includes errorless learning, immediate feedback, and kinesthetic activities.

Re-teaching or Pre-teaching?

If you are a classroom teacher, you know about re-teaching a concept or skill to students who didn't "get it" when it was taught to the whole class. These students were "lost."

The usual procedure is to take these students and work with them in a small group *after* the initial instruction. Many times in this focused, small group setting, these students begin to understand. Think about it. They did not learn the first time, but it was the second encounter that taught them. In other words, they were only taught once. The first time doesn't count.

Whole Class ⟶ Small Group

A more powerful approach to consider is pre-teaching. You know which students usually have difficulty. Take these students and teach the concept or skill to them in a small group *before* the initial instruction.

Small Group ⟶ Whole Class

Then when students are instructed in the whole group, the concept or skill is being reinforced. They understand it from the previous work in the small group. They are now being taught twice: the first time in a small group and the second time with the whole class. This approach produces significantly better results.

Strategies for Kinesthetic Learners	How it Meets the Need
☐ Writing on white boards ☐ Manipulating flash cards, activity cards, or 3x5 cards ☐ Manipulating objects ☐ Performing demonstrations and experiments ☐ Working on the computer ☐ Engaging in small group discussions ☐ Dramatizing ☐ Playing games	Engages the large muscles The student, not the teacher, manipulates the cards, performs the demonstrations, etc.
☐ Diagrams ☐ Graphic organizers ☐ Pictures	Helps them see the big picture Helps them organize bits and pieces of information
☐ Problem-solving ☐ Evaluating	Satisfies the need to know why
☐ Creative projects	Satisfies the need to be creative
☐ Teacher brings in objects ☐ Field trips ☐ Simulations	Helps them form a 3-dimensional picture of the concept in their mind

Chapter 4: The Discovery that Changes Everything!

Insanity: doing the same thing over and over again and expecting different results.

-- Albert Einstein

The discovery that changes everything!

For over 100 years, it was assumed that we read by seeing and remembering words. The *Look-Say* method in the *Dick and Jane* series, the whole word method, and the whole language movement all reflect that understanding. Although some aspects of each of these approaches differ, the basic philosophy is the same. Students are taught to look at a word as a whole and remember it without giving much attention to individual letters or sounds. They memorize the words.

Then came brain research. During the past thirty years, neuroscientists from top universities all over the world have made amazing discoveries about the reading process. When they "looked" into the brain with neuroimaging equipment to see what happens when we read, ***they were surprised!***

By observing the activity in the brain, they learned not only what *skills* need to be taught, but also the *order* in which they should be taught. Most of these findings are so well-documented that there is no argument as to their value. These results are just now starting to trickle into our reading curriculums with more yet to come.

How the brain processes words

So how do we read? Sound by sound. Good readers rapidly perceive every letter in every word. They process words in the language centers on the **left side** of the brain in a ***specific*** sequence, averaging five or more words per second.

Speech Sound Center ▶ Letter Center ▶ Word Center

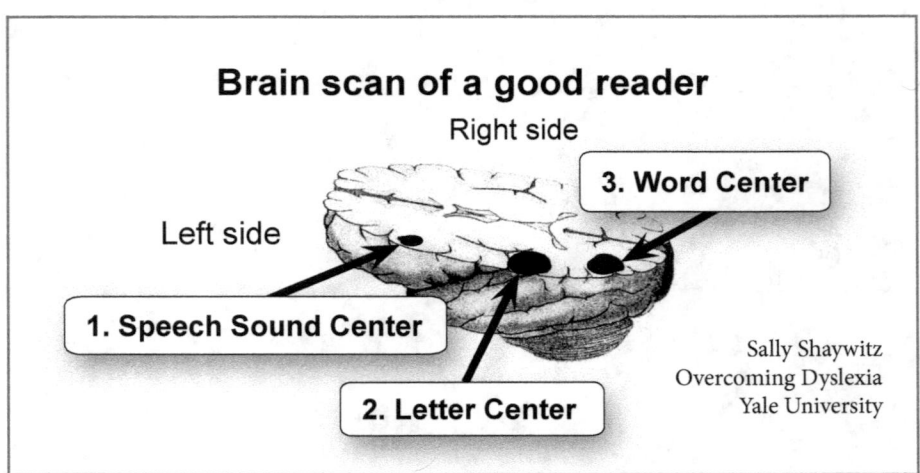

Sally Shaywitz
Overcoming Dyslexia
Yale University

1. **Speech Sound Center** *(Broca's area of the brain)*

    The Speech Sound Center is the first area of the brain that "fires." It is located in the left front of the brain and stores the *42-44 *speech* sounds of our language. Good readers are able to break ***spoken*** words into the individual speech sounds and use that skill to read words.

    No one knew that the ability to hear the individual sounds in ***spoken*** words had anything to do with reading! In fact, scientists and other researchers discovered that a person must be able to break a ***spoken*** word into the individual sounds to be a good reader, no matter how old they may be. Poor readers cannot do this. They may know the alphabet, but they struggle with reading because they are missing this skill.

    *NOTE: The number of speech sounds you use will depend on where you live. Your accent determines the number of sounds used.

    ---
    *A person must be able to break a **spoken** word into individual sounds to be a good reader.*

    ---

2. **Letter Center** *(Parieto-temporal area of the brain)*

    The second area of the brain to "fire" is the Letter Center. The brain rapidly associates the sounds with the letter or letters that represent them. This area communicates with the Speech Sound Center and the Word Center to support word recognition.

    That means a good reader knows more than just the 26 letters of the alphabet. They must know all the letter combinations that represent each of the 42-44 sounds such as *ng, tch, ie, igh* and *ck*.

    A person must know all the letter combinations that represent each of the 42-44 speech sounds.

    ---

3. **Word Center** *(Occipital-temporal area of the brain)*

    This is the third center that "fires." After a word has been processed using the first two language centers, it is stored with its *structure* and *meaning* in this area. We say it has been "phonologically processed." In other words, attention has been given to :

- The sounds
- How those sounds are represented with letters
- The structure which includes prefixes and suffixes
- Meaning of the word

Words stored here can be retrieved instantly.

The right content and the right sequence

Neuroscientists and researchers have made it easy for us. We now know the right content and the right sequence to teach reading. We can use this knowledge as the foundation to select the right curriculum and to assess struggling readers. This becomes a checklist of "what you need to know." If anything is missing in a curriculum, we need to add it or choose another curriculum. If a reader is missing any skill, then we need to teach it.

The sequence is important, too. We want to teach reading in the same order the brain processes words. For some students with visual, auditory, and tactile learning styles, it may not be quite as important. But to a kinesthetic learner, it is essential. The following checklist identifies the *right content* in the *right sequence* with the *right instruction.*

The Right Instruction	• Errorless learning and immediate feedback • Confidence that students can achieve • Kinesthetic strategies for every concept.
The Right Content	• Hear the individual sounds in spoken words • Know the spellings of the 42-44 speech sounds • Put sounds and spellings together to form words • Know how to add prefixes and suffixes • Be able to decode small and big words • Read smoothly with expression • Think about meaning
The Right Sequence	• The sequence the brain uses in processing words

*Students must know how words are formed,
know how to decode them
and understand the meaning of the words.*

How do poor readers read?

Quite differently. Brain scans of struggling readers show they do not process words on the left side of the brain, but activate the ***right*** side.

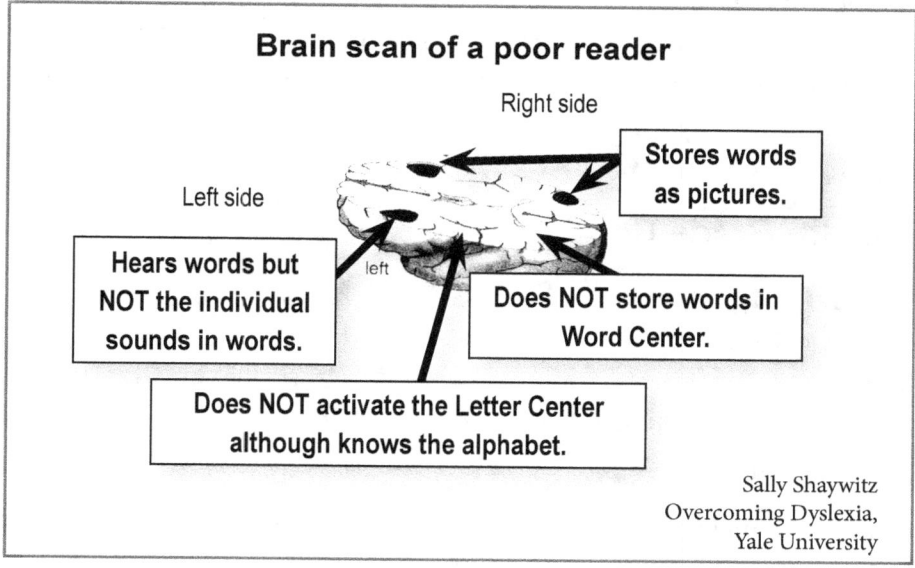

Sally Shaywitz
Overcoming Dyslexia,
Yale University

The Speech Sound Center is activated, but only because the individual is trying to pronounce the word. Even when the student knows the alphabet, the Letter Center is not used because the letters have not been associated with the speech sound. Struggling readers do not understand the underlying sound structure of words and that prevents the words from being stored in the Word Center. Instead, the shape of the word and meaning are stored on the right side of the brain. Words are stored as pictures.

If words are processed on the right side of the brain, they have been stored *without* all of the information necessary for instant retrieval. Here are the problems with words stored on the ***right*** side of the brain.

- **Words are retrieved inefficiently and more slowly.**

    Since words are not stored in the Word Center, they cannot be retrieved instantly. These individuals usually read word by word and very laboriously. Some have labeled it "word calling."

- **Reading is not fluent.**

    Since it takes so much effort just to read the words, fluency is difficult. It is a common practice to have these students read and reread a text until they know the words from memory in order to achieve a semblance of fluency. However, this is not true fluency.

- **Comprehension is usually poor.**

    It takes so much effort just to read the words that there is little working memory left to process the meaning. What is working memory? It is the memory that *temporarily* holds only the information we are currently using. And it has a limited capacity. You can only think about so many things at one time. It differs from short-term and long-term memory.

The 4th Grade Crash

Ben, my third grade student, performed well in my classroom. He produced excellent work and showed no signs of any kind of learning problems whatsoever. For this reason, I was stunned to learn that by 5th grade he could not read well enough to complete his school work and had to receive remedial help in reading. What happened?

I have heard many teachers report this same phenomenon. As one teacher said, "I couldn't believe it! She was just fine in my class. How could she suddenly not be able to read?" Look at the chart. Students appear to be gaining reading skills during first, second, and third grade, and then suddenly the achievement plummets. What happened?

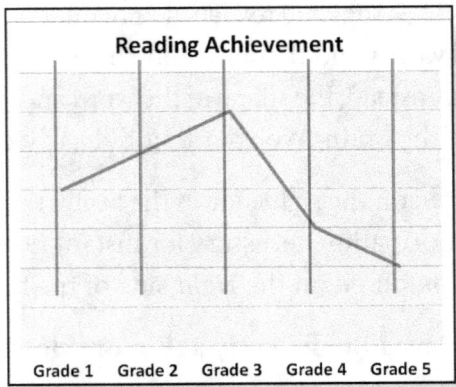

To find the answer, we have to revisit how the brain reads. Proficient readers have processed words through the language centers of the brain and have stored them with all of the associated data in the back of the brain where they can be instantly retrieved. In contrast, the language centers of poor readers are not activated during reading. Instead, right brain networks compensate for the inability to analyze and process words properly. Students have not stored words with all of the associated sound and structure data, but as pictures. The bottom line questions then become:

1. How well could these students read in the first place? How did they "get by" with their limited skills?
2. How many words can they memorize using the right brain networks instead of the language centers of the left brain? At what point are there too many words?

How well could these readers read in the first place?

If we could crawl into the mind of these readers, we would be amazed at the compensation skills used to read texts. Since early childhood, they have been exposed to the concept of story. Even if parents never read to them, they have watched movies that have characters, settings, and plots. Each story has a problem and finally a resolution. They understand *story*.

You will be surprised how easy it is for you to read the following story. All primary texts include pictures that give substantial clues to the reader.

The hoρσε is ρυννινγ. The hoρσε wαvτσ to go hoμε.

This hoρσε bελονγσ to a yουνγ girl thατ λιϖεσ doων the stρεετ fρομ my gρανδμοτηερ. This hoρσε is a Σπανιsη σταλλιον.

The only words that will trip you up are gρανδμοτηερ and Σταλλιον. You will guess at gρανδμοτηερ and come close. On Σταλλιον, you are stumped unless you are familiar with horses. But because all of the other words are within your knowledge base and vocabulary, you will do a

45

good job at guessing and reading. Remember, the struggling reader has not processed words through the language centers so individual letters are not that significant. See the translation of the story in Appendix D.

Now the student has entered 5th grade and must read longer and more complex texts without pictures. What are the differences between reading this text and the story about the horse?

> The εξχιτεμεντ of these last μανευϖερσ had σομεωηατ ιντερφερεδ with the watch I had kept ηιτηερτο, sharply enough, upon the χοξσωαιν. Even then I was still much ιντερεστεδ, waiting for the ship to touch, χρανινγ over the σταρβοαρδ βυλωαρκσ and watching the ριππλεσ spreading wide before the bows.

If you were a student attempting to read this, what feelings and thoughts would be going through your mind? One 6th grade student said to me, "I can't read enough words in a sentence to even know what the sentence is talking about."

Poor readers lack the skills to decode unknown words.

The concepts and the vocabulary are beyond the everyday experience of students. As they enter 4th grade, they are suddenly faced with stories and informational texts with unknown vocabulary. They are not able to memorize enough words to keep up with the demands.

Why some poor readers succeed better than others

Although, poor readers do not process words through the left brain language centers, some do better than others. It depends on several factors including what they have been taught about reading, their vocabulary development, and their ability to memorize. But all struggle with reading.

- **Vocabulary development**

    One of the factors that contributes to better success is vocabulary development. Through exposure to a wide range of experiences and conversations about those experiences, students gain vocabulary knowledge. If an individual understands a concept and the vocabulary that goes with it, then the chances of figuring out a text with those words and concepts is more likely. As students grow older, they may seem to function fairly well, even though they struggled with reading during the early years.

However, brain imaging reveals that these individuals are still not processing words in the language centers of the brain. They may be fairly accurate readers, but they are usually slow readers and comprehension often suffers. They usually avoid reading.

- **Incredible memory**

    Another factor is an incredible memory. One of my colleagues who was completing her doctorate degree confessed that she could not figure out a word on her own. Amazingly, if someone told her the word, she remembered it forever.

    Kevin, a student who had just finished his junior year in high school struggled to maintain "C's." The school had determined he did not have a reading problem because he was an adequate reader and so labeled him "writing disabled" due to deficiencies in that area.

    However, the *Woodcock Reading Mastery Test* along with other tests revealed he was reading at a beginning 6th grade level, *five grade levels below his grade*. To do as well as he had in school, he had memorized thousands of words and could conceptually understand the contexts of those words. When he was taught the right content in the right sequence with the right instruction, he started processing words in the language centers of the brain and was able to earn "A's" and "B's" his senior year.

How the brain can change

As I was teaching these poor readers, I noticed they began to instantly recognize words after a few lessons. Their reading became smooth. It appeared that they were now processing words in the language centers of the left brain, but I had no way to look into their brains to see what was happening. Then Yale University provided the proof through their studies.

Notice the Speech Sound Center is activated because the student is attempting to pronounce the word. The other languages centers of the left side of the brain are *not* activated. Words are being processed on the **right** side of the brain.

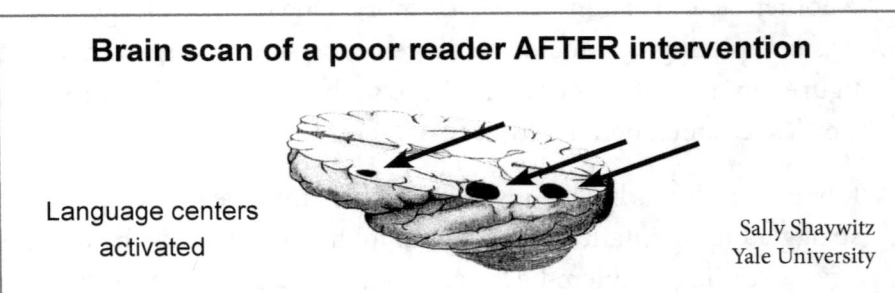

Look at the changes in the brain after intervention. Notice that *all* processing is now on the ***left*** side with *none* on the right. Amazing!

If students are *not* using the language centers of the left brain, they are left with only two options for learning to read:

- Memorize words
- Guess words

Neither option results in a proficient reader.

Skills of low-performing readers

What do low-performing readers know? What don't they know? We do not want to spend time on skills they have, but we want to concentrate on those they do not have.

- **They usually know the letters of the alphabet**

    Kindergarten and Grade 1 students may not know the alphabet. However, those in Grades 2 and up usually know the entire alphabet.

If you are working with a K-1 student, check to see how much of the alphabet they know.

- **They usually know the most common sounds of letters**

    Students in Grades 2 and up usually know the common sounds of the consonants such as *c* saying /k/, but usually do not know uncommon sounds such as the c that can say /s/ or the *g* that can say /j/.

- **They know small words they have memorized**

    Students in Grades 2 and up may have memorized words such as *could, should, were, was,* and *there*. This allows them to read texts that have letters and letter combinations you have not taught them. Always check the reading level so you know what words students know. Some older students may only know a handful of words.

- **Some students may have memorized many words.**

    Some students may be able to read texts at middle elementary levels, but if they are in high school, they are still reading several grade levels below their grade. A high school student reading at 5th grade level can't read well enough to do well in school. Some may have memorized enough words to get along fairly well in high school, but they do not like to read and read very slowly.

What poor readers usually DO NOT know

- **They do not know some vowel sounds and vowel spellings.**

    They often cannot distinguish the differences between some of the short vowel sounds such as /ĭ/ and /ĕ/. For example, many times they cannot hear the difference between the middle sounds of words like *Ben* and *bin*. They definitely do not know how to spell the long vowel sounds and they do not know the spellings or the sounds of the vowel sounds /oi/, /ou/, /au/, and /o͝o/.

- **They do not know consonant spellings such as *tch, ph, dge,* and *ng*.**

    Although they know the letters of the alphabet, they usually do not know many of the letter combinations used in our language. When they see combinations like *th, sh*, or *tch*, they may try to pronounce each letter individually such as /t/ and /ch/ when they see *tch*. They usually do not know that *gn* says /n/ or that *dge* says /j/.

- **They do not know that words are spelled according to the sounds of speech.**

    They often do not know there is any relationship between the sounds in a spoken word and the letters that represent it on paper. They do not have any idea there is any connection.

    A fifteen year old student jumped out of his chair and exclaimed, "I get it! I get it!" I wasn't sure what he got. "What did you get?" So he explained for the word *map*. "I get that /m/ is the *m* and /a/ is the *a* and /p/ is the *p*." Until this point, the letters in words were completely arbitrary. He had no idea there was any relationship between the sounds in a spoken word and the letters on a page.

- **They do not know that words are made up of individual sounds.**

    They cannot break a word apart into its individual sounds. When they attempt to do so, they run the sounds together.

- **They may not know the difference between some consonant sounds.**

    They confuse sounds such as /b/ and /p/, /f/ and /v/, /ch/ and /j/ and sometimes represent these with the incorrect letter. These pairs are explained in the next chapter.

You have the tools

You now know what tools are needed to teach reading. We will discuss these in detail in the following chapters.

- *The right instruction* is using errorless learning, immediate feedback, and kinesthetic strategies with confidence that students can be successful.
- *The right content* was discovered by neuroscientists and researchers. This is what students need to be able to do:
    1. Hear the individual sounds in spoken words
    2. Know the spellings of the 42 - 44 speech sounds
    3. Put sounds and spellings together to form words
    4. Know how to add prefixes and suffixes
    5. Be able to decode small and big words
    6. Read smoothly with expression
    7. Think about meaning
- *The right sequence* is using the same sequence the brain uses in processing words.

Chapter 5: The Secret to Hearing Sounds in Spoken Words

The ability to hear individual sounds in spoken words is the critical predictor of the ability to read well.

other states, you will only use 42 sounds. For example, words like *daughter* and *car* are pronounced differently in different parts of the United States.

A speech sound is called a phoneme.

Phonemes are represented with slash marks (/ /) on either side of the letter or letters. This distinguishes them from letters. The following is how we represent phonemes (speech sounds).

/t/   /d/   /th/

Phoneme awareness

Phonemic awareness is the ability to hear and manipulate the individual sounds in **spoken** words. When we say the word *stand*, students must be able to hear the five individual sounds /s/, /t/, /a/ , /n/, /d/ in that word. During conversation, we only attend to words as a whole, but to be a proficient reader, we must be able to segment the spoken word into the individual sounds.

Phonemic awareness is the ability
to hear and manipulate the individual sounds in spoken words.

Struggling readers, whether they are seven or seventy, have limited phonemic awareness. They are not able to hear the individual sounds in spoken words. Since this is the first area of the brain that "fires" when words are processed properly, the rest of the sequence will also fail. Words cannot be processed in the language centers of the left brain if an individual cannot hear the sounds of speech.

Awareness of phonemes is so important to reading
that those who don't have it will struggle with reading.

Levels of Phonemic Awareness

Phonemic awareness, the awareness of the individual sounds in spoken words, isn't "you have it or you don't have it." There are different levels of understanding that students acquire over time. As a teacher, you need to understand each of these levels so you can monitor student growth. At all times, you need to know at which level each student is functioning.

Here are the six level of phonemic awareness listed in the order of difficulty and in the order which most students learn them.

Six Levels of Phonemic Awareness

Level 1: Hear beginning sound
Level 2: Hear end sound
Level 3: Hear middle vowel sound
Level 4: Hear all sounds
Level 5: Manipulate sounds
Level 6: Blend sounds together

The older students I teach can usually hear the beginning sound in a spoken word even if they can only read a handful of words. However, they often do not have any of the other five levels of phonemic awareness. Younger students who struggle with reading may not even have this first level.

Continually monitor the phonemic awareness level of each student.

Level 1: Hear beginning sound.

I can hear /s/ in the word sand.

When given a word orally, students can tell you the sound they hear at the beginning of the word. For example, if you say the word *sand*, they can tell you the beginning sound is /s/.

This is usually the easiest sound for students to hear in a word, but sometimes students who have hearing problems hear the end sound more easily than the beginning sound.

Level 2: Hear end sound

I can hear /s/ and /d/ in the word sand.

The end sound is usually the next easiest sound for students to hear. Once they hear the beginning sound, they need to start listening for the end sound.

Level 3: Hear middle vowel sound

I can hear /s/ - /a/ and /d/ in the word sand.

At this level, students hear the beginning, end, and now the middle vowel sound of words. However, they still may not hear all of the sounds in a word. For example, given the word *sand*, they can tell you the beginning, end, and the middle vowel sound /a/, but they do not hear the /n./ If the middle sound is a short vowel, students may have difficulty distinguishing between the sounds, such the difference between the short vowel sounds in *pen* and *pin*.

Level 4: Hear all sounds

I can hear /s/ - /a/ - /n/ - /d/ in the word sand.

At this level of sophistication, students can hear and segment all of the phonemes in a word. They hear each individual sound in words like *computer* and *international*.

Level 5: Manipulate sounds

I can change /s/ to /b/ to change sand to band.

At this level, students understand how adding or deleting sounds in a word changes it to a new word. This skill usually comes quickly after Level 4. They are able to understand the relationship between *wage* and *stage*, seeing the need to only change the beginning letters.

Level 6: Blend sounds together

I can blend the sounds of sand together to say the word.

This skill is used when constructing words. Students are able to segment the sounds in a spoken word, write the spelling of each sound, and then blend them back together to say the word again. They understand how phonemes blend together to form words.

Voiced and unvoiced sounds

The following consonant pairs are formed in the mouth in the same way, but one sound is voiced (uses the voice box) and the other sound is whispered without the voice. Try saying each pair and notice how you form the sound in your mouth. Then notice what it feels like to use the voice box.

Unvoiced	Voiced	Unvoiced example	Voiced example
/p/	/b/	poor	bore
/s/	/z/	loose	lose
/f/	/v/	file	vile
/th/	/th/	thin	then
/t/	/d/	to	do
/ch/	/j/	cheer	jeer
/k/	/g/	cold	gold
/sh/	/zh/	mission	vision
/wh/	/w/	whale	wait

The difficulty with voiced and unvoiced sounds

- *Some readers may confuse these sounds.* Children just learning to read, those with speech or hearing impairments, and struggling readers often confuse these sounds. They can confuse them when they say or write words using these sounds. As you teach the graphemes, have students think about how the sounds are formed in the mouth and how they add the voice to the sound.

- *The way we spell and pronounce some words is confusing.* The voiced and unvoiced pairs may be used interchangeably.

/s/ - /z/

An *s* at the end of a word 0can be pronounced /s/ or /z/ as in the words *likes* and *was*.

/f/ - /v/

The letter *f* is changed to a *v* when forming the plural in several words, such as *wife* to *wives* and *leaf* to *leaves*. The word *of* uses the voiced /v/ instead of the unvoiced /f/ because it would be almost impossible to use the unvoiced /f/. Try saying the word *of* using the unvoiced /f/ sound.

/t/ - /d/

The phonemes /d/ and /t/ are exchanged in many words. For example, it is often difficult to tell which sound is used in words such as *letter, ladder,* and *little*. This interchange also explains why the suffix _ed can say /d/, /t/, or /uhd/. Listen to the suffix as you say the words *changed* (/d/), *jumped* (/t/, *parted* (/uhd/).

/wh/ - /w/

The phoneme /wh/ is disappearing from our language and the voiced pair /w/ is sometimes used instead. When saying a word like *whale* or *when*, do you feel a puff of air when you hold your hand in front of your mouth? Some individuals do and some don't. The younger you are, the more likely you don't. In time, the *wh* might be just another grapheme to represent the phoneme /w/.

Use caution in pronouncing sounds

When pronouncing some of the consonant sounds, it is easy to drag out the sound by adding /uh/ at the end. If we say /buh/ instead of the short staccato /b/, it makes it impossible to blend sounds together to form a word such as *bat*. *Buh-at* isn't a word. Here are the sounds to pronounce with caution. Say these sounds as short as possible like a hot potato.

/b/	/c/	/d/	/g/	/h/	/j/	/k/
/p/	/q/	/r/	/t/	/v/	/w/	/y/

In Summary

1. A phoneme is a speech sound. It is NOT the sound a letter makes.

2. Awareness of phonemes in spoken words is a critical skill in learning to read well.

3. Students who do not have phonemic awareness will struggle with reading.

4. There are six levels of phonemic awareness. Be able to identify which levels a student has and does not have.

5. Some students will have difficulty with voiced and unvoiced pairs. Help them distinguish the differences in these sounds.

6. When pronouncing some of the consonant sounds, avoid dragging out the sound by adding /uh/ at the end.

Chapter 6:
The Secret to Teaching Phonemic Awareness

Phonemic awareness is an auditory skill that must be taught with all four learning styles.

Guidelines for phonemic awareness activities

Phonemic awareness is a new concept in reading instruction so it is taking time for us to get it right. There are activities labeled phonemic awareness *that are not* phonemic awareness activities. Be careful! There are also phonemic awareness activities that do not produce the results we want, especially for the kinesthetic learner. These guidelines will ensure that you are truly teaching phonemic awareness and that you are meeting the needs of all sensory learning styles, including the kinesthetic learner.

- **Start with the spoken word.**

    Give words orally. Any activity that provides students with a written word or a letter is *not* a phonemic awareness activity.

- **The student, not the teacher, isolates the sound.**

    Students, and not the teacher, must segment the sound. Any activity where the teacher segments the sound from a spoken word for the students is *not* a phonemic awareness activity. For example, if the teacher asks students to find objects that begin with the sound /b/, it is not a phonemic awareness activity. Instead, the teacher asks, "What sound do you hear at the beginning of *basket*?" The student then isolates the sound.

- **Students listen only for individual sounds in words, not groups of sounds.**

    Any activity that asks students to listen for rhymes, syllables, or other groups of sounds is *not* a phonemic awareness activity. A phonemic awareness activity will always ask students to segment or manipulate *individual* sounds in spoken words.

- **Students identify the letters represented by the sound.**

    Researchers have found that connecting the speech sound to the written representation of that sound is significantly more effective than just having students listen and only respond orally. If students respond with sound cards, tiles, or white boards, they are identifying the letters that represent the sound, strengthening the connection between the Speech Sound Center and the Letter Center of the brain. The exception are activities specifically for students in Grades 2 and up. These students should also *engage in activities that require them to listen for the sounds without finding the letter representations.* This prevents them from depending upon their knowledge of spelling and forces them to focus on hearing the individual sounds. The Chip Game is an example of this type of activity. It is described later in this chapter.

- **Use all four sensory learning styles.**

    If students use whiteboards, tiles, or sound cards, they are using all four learning styles.

    - They *hear* the word.
    - They *say* the sound.
    - They *see* the representation of the sound on a card.
    - They *respond* using tactile and kinesthetic methods.

    This addresses the needs of all learning styles, including the kinesthetic learners.

- **Students respond individually in a tangible way.**

    The strongest phonemic awareness activity will require an individual, tangible response in addition to the oral reply. When the teacher says a word, students will say the isolated sound and also manipulate cards, objects, or write on the white board to show that sound. This provides immediate feedback to the teacher as to what each student knows and does not know.

    Phonemic activities that *only* require an oral response or a group kinesthetic response will *not* provide the information you need to know about the progress of each student. Also, if students respond orally as a group, the struggling readers, the ones who need this instruction the most, will just "follow the leader." They usually are not learning from the activity.

Phonemic Awareness: Sound Cards

This activity focuses on Phonemic Awareness Levels 1 - 3 and can be done with different letters or letter combinations and up to eight cards at once. It meets all six of the guidelines for a phonemic awareness activity. You can use capital and lowercase letters, just the lowercase letters, or cards with all the possible spellings of the sound. Here are examples of the different types of cards that can be used for different age or ability levels.

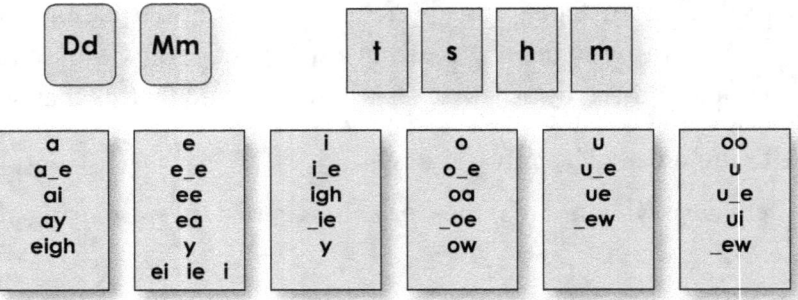

> Teacher: "I have given each of you one Dd and one Mm card. I will say a word and then you say it back to me. If the word ends with the /d/ sound, hold up the Dd letter card. If the word ends with the /Mm/ sound, hold up the Mm card. Say the sound when you hold up the card."
>
> Teacher: "What sound do you hear at the end of *ride*?"
>
> Children: "*ride*"
>
> Children: (Hold up the Dd letter card) "/d/"
>
> Words to use:
>
> | broom | add | find | glad | seem |
> |-------|-----|------|------|------|
> | grade | need | swim | hide | room |

Keep the game fast-paced

This game is fast-paced, taking only a few minutes for students to respond to several words. Establish a rhythm.

1. **Ask for the beginning, middle, or end sound of a spoken word.**

   This game requires students to hear the individual sounds in words and to connect that sound to the letter representation.

2. **Ask students to point to the correct spelling when ready**

   As students advance in their skills, you will ask them to show you the correct spelling after they have found the card and said the sound. For example, students have just studied that *ck* comes only after a short vowel and the word you say is *track*. After they have chosen the c card and said /c/, ask them to point to the correct spelling (ck).

Chapter 6 / Teaching Phonemic Awareness

3. **Always give immediate and corrective feedback.**

    If students don't know which letter represents the sound, show them. Be discrete and nonchalant about it. As students choose a card, help any who are having difficulty finding the correct one. Discretely point to the right card if they begin picking up the wrong one. The goal is to have students choose the right card and say the correct sound.

4. **Provide extra practice with sounds they continue having difficulty distinguishing.**

    Beginning readers and those just learning the language may need more practice with sounds they have difficulty distinguishing such as the short /ĕ/ from the short /ĭ/ or the difference between voiced and unvoiced pairs. If they have not learned to distinguish these within five or six lessons, take time to show them the difference in how they are formed in the mouth. Then use only those two cards so they practice hearing the difference between the sounds.

5. **Keep in mind that short vowel sounds are difficult to hear and long vowel sounds are difficult to spell.**

    Short vowel sounds are the most difficult to hear because there is little difference in the way they are formed in the mouth. You may have to stop and have students notice how their mouth and tongue change when they say each sound.

    Long vowels are usually easier to hear but they have many more spellings. Poor readers can usually hear long vowel spellings, but you should use these sound cards anyway so student get used to seeing the different ways to spell the sound.

Special instructions for Kindergarten and Grade 1

This game should be played with all children in this age group in a small group setting. If you are working with young beginning readers who are at risk, they will need extra practice. Here are some guidelines.

Choose only the letters that these children have been taught. Practice sounds they have difficulty hearing such as /t/ at the beginning of *train*, /d/ at the beginning of *dress*. Stretch out the words if necessary to help them hear the sounds.

Follow the sequence of phonemic awareness levels. Start with Phonemic Awareness Level 1, listening for the beginning sound in words. When students can usually hear the beginning sound, then introduce Level 2, listening for the end sound in words. Lastly, introduce listening for the middle vowel sound in words.

Special instructions for Grades 2 and up

Use the instructions for Kindergarten - Grade 1 except adjust the content for the older grades. Almost all struggling readers in these grades know the alphabet and can hear the beginning sound in words. They can often hear the end sounds in many words. This is true even if they can read only a handful of words. If you have a student in these grades that does not know the alphabet, then follow all of the guidelines for K- Grade 1.

- **Ask students to point to the correct spelling**

    After teaching the spellings of a particular vowel sound or consonant, ask students to point to the correct spelling after they have chosen the card and said the sound.

    "What sound do you hear at the end of sludge? Which spelling is it? "

- **Use cards for the consonants they cannot hear.**

    Only a few students may need practice hearing the beginning and end sounds of the more common consonants such as *b, d, f, g, h*, etc. Use cards for any consonants they cannot hear.

- **Use cards for more difficult consonant spellings.**

    These are the spellings these students usually don't know and often can't hear. Use cards to help students associate the beginning and end sounds of words with the spellings of these more difficult consonant spellings. The book *The "Real Rules" of English*™ explains each spelling and how they are used.

j	c	sh	x	z	ng	wh	ch	qu
g(e)	k	ti		_s	_n_		tch	
g(i)	ck	si						
g(y)	ch	ci		x_				
dge	_que	ch						

- **Focus on the vowel sounds.**

    Vowels sounds are a problem for most poor readers. They have difficulty hearing them as well as spelling them. They rarely know the sounds or the spellings of the vowel sounds /oi/, /au/, /ou/, and /ar/. They need a significant amount of practice with these. Here are the spellings of the vowel sounds they need to know.

ă	ĕ ea	ĭ	ŏ	ŭ ȧ ė ȯ _ou_	oŏ u
ā a_e ai ay eigh	ē e_e ee ea y	ī i_e igh _ie y	ō o_e oa ow	ū u_e _ue _ew	oō u_e _ue u ui ew
oi oy	au aw a	ou ow	ar		

Phonemic Awareness: Chip Game

This kinesthetic phonemic awareness game is designed for students in Grades 2 and up and is *not* recommended for younger students because it does *not* connect the speech sound with the letter representations. We want younger students to consistently play phonemic awareness games that connect the sound with the letter or letters that represent it.

This activity focuses on Phonemic Awareness Levels 4 and 6. Students must listen for all the sounds in a spoken word. You will hear students whispering each sound as they lay out the chips. You will also hear them blending those sounds together to form the word.

Colored chips are used to represent the speech sound so these older students are forced to listen for the sounds in spoken words rather than lean on their knowledge of spelling. They have to be reminded that they are not spelling the word, but putting down a chip for every *sound* they hear. You can use any type of chips. You just need two colors. They can be two-sided chips or single colored chips.

In my experience, all ages like this game. It is a challenge, and yet there is immediate corrective feedback so each word is completed correctly. There are "high fives" not only among students but teachers who are learning this game. Here are the guidelines and what students will learn.

- **Choose words within the vocabulary of students.**

    Choose words that students know, but most likely do not know how to spell. Make sure the words are challenging enough with four or more sounds. Only four words per game are necessary.

- **Use the principles of errorless learning and immediate feedback.**

    After initially putting down the chips, students correct any errors. This is critical. After they have fixed the errors and the chips are correct, they say each sound as they move each chip up. This gives them practice hearing each individual sound

- **Students learn how to identify individual sounds in words.**

    Most students can usually identify the first one or two sounds in a word, but then put down an arbitrary number of chips thereafter. The word may have six sounds but they may put down two, five, or even ten chips because they have no idea how to segment the sounds of a word. They learn, though, how to segment through this game.

- **Students learn the difference between vowels and consonants.**

    Some students will not know the difference between a vowel sound and a consonant sound when they first play this game. The process of laying down the proper color of chip and then saying the sound helps them learn the difference.

I played this game twice a week with poor readers who had no idea how many sounds were in any given word. In about ten lessons, most of them could put down the chips perfectly without any help. This game provides kinesthetic learners with the large muscle movement necessary for optimal learning. Students also receive immediate feedback during the game so the task is completed without error.

Chip Game Example

> Materials: Each student has fifteen colored counting chips that are gray on one side and white on the other.
>
>
>
> Teacher: "The gray chips are consonants; the white chips are vowels. I will say a word and you will put down a chip for every sound you hear in the word. You will *not* be spelling the word—only putting down a chip for every *sound*. If it is a consonant, put down a gray chip. If it is a vowel sound, put down a white chip.
>
> Teacher: "Lay down a chip for each sound you hear in *brother*."
>
> Students: (*Students put down a chip for each sound.*)
>
> ● ● ○ ● ●
> /b/-/r/-/o/-/th/-/r/
>
> Teacher: (*To one student*) "Say each sound as you point to each chip. Everyone fix any chips that are not correct." *Student says each sound when pointing to each chip. If the chip is incorrect, then the correct one is put down. Every student makes any corrections necessary.*
>
> Teacher: (*To all students*) "Now let's say each sound as you slide each chip up."
>
> All students: (*Students say each sound as they push each chip up.*)
>
> Words to use:
>
>   computer   nicely   thinking   stronger

Try it!

Read the words below and count the number of phonemes you hear. Remember, it is not the number of letters in a word, but the number of sounds. Write down the number and then check the answers in Appendix D.

    bringing   station   thing
    hopeless   institution   packing

Phonemic Awareness Assessments

Before working with a student, determine the phonemic awareness skills by administering assessments. You need to know what the student knows and doesn't know. *Be careful.* The ability to read is *not* a sign that a student has phonemic awareness because students may have memorized words, processing them on the right side of the brain.

The opposite can also be true. A student who cannot read may have phonemic awareness skills but does not know how to spell those sounds or how to decode words. The student may have fairly good phonemic awareness, but is missing the next set of skills.

When choosing phonemic awareness assessments ask two questions:
1. Is it truly a test of phonemic awareness?
2. Does it provide a tangible way to respond?

Phonemic awareness is a relatively new idea to education and for that reason there are "phonemic awareness" assessments that *are not* actually tests of phonemic awareness. Use the same guidelines for an assessment as you do for an activity to determine if it is a true test of phonemic awareness with a tangible way of responding.

Some assessments can be tweaked to meet all of the requirements. For example, if the assessment asks only for an oral response to determine how many sounds are in a word, you can require the student to place chips or tiles down for each sound and then tell you how many sounds they hear. You may not get an accurate assessment if the student only responds by saying each sound individually. It is easy for a student to stretch the sounds so it is difficult to tell whether the word was actually segmented or if the word was just stretched out. Was it /d/- /o/-/g/ or was it d. . . o. . . g?

If the teacher asks the student to find a picture that begins with /t/, it is *not* a test of phonemic awareness because the teacher has segmented the sound. The student must be the one identifying the sound at the beginning, end, or middle of an object or word. If the teacher shows a picture and asks what sound they hear at the beginning, then it *is* a test of phonemic awareness.

If you are working with students individually or in a small group, you will find it easy to monitor the growth in phonemic awareness levels. You can record when they can hear the beginning, end, and middle sounds of words. You will be able to observe when they are able to segment, blend, and manipulate sounds. Any formal testing done after a few weeks of instruction will only verify what you have already documented. Phonemic awareness assessments are found in Chapter 16 along with other assessments.

Chapter 7: The Secret to Spelling Sounds

The purpose of the alphabet is to make spoken words visible.

-- Jeanine Herron, 2010

Hearing the individual sounds in words and knowing the letter representations of those sounds are the foundational skills for learning to read. These skills are necessary for words to be processed and stored in the Word Center of the brain where they can be retrieved instantly.

Speech Sound Center ▶ Letter Center ▶ Word Center

The Right Instruction	• Errorless learning and immediate feedback • Confidence that students can achieve • Kinesthetic strategies for every concept.
The Right Content	• Hear the individual sounds in spoken words • **Know the spellings of the 42-44 speech sounds** • Put sounds and spellings together to form words • Know how to add prefixes and suffixes • Be able to decode small and big words • Read smoothly with expression • Think about meaning
The Right Sequence	• The sequence the brain uses in processing words

The spellings of the speech sounds

There are 127 ways to spell the 42-44 sounds of speech. Some of these spellings are found in just a few words; others are found in many words. These spellings follow very specific patterns and rules. When I was teaching first grade students, by the time I had taught about 50 of these spellings, they could read words with many of the other spellings because the patterns are so predictable.

The spellings of speech sounds are called *graphemes* which comes from the Greek root *graph*, meaning "to write." A grapheme is a letter or a letter combination that represent a speech sound (phoneme). When we use the term alphabet, we are referring to the 26 letters of the alphabet. When we use the term grapheme, we are referring to all the representations of a speech sound, *including the letters of the alphabet*. A list of all the graphemes are found in Appendix A. Here are some examples.

Phoneme (speech sound)	Grapheme
/g/	g or gu
/ch/	ch or tch
/ng/	ng or _n

The graphemes are stored in the Letter Center of the brain. If students do not know the graphemes, that information is missing in that center. The brain cannot attach a grapheme to the speech sound and the reading process fails.

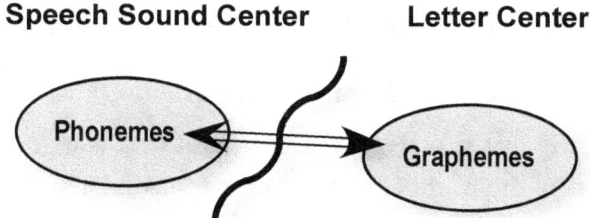

That is why any beginning reader must be taught these graphemes. First graders should know most of the 127 graphemes by the end of the year. Struggling readers in Grades 2 and up usually know the alphabet, but they need access as quickly as possible to the rest of the graphemes. My older elementary and high school students were taught these graphemes in 45 one-hour lessons.

What you need to know about graphemes

English has the reputation of being a difficult language to learn, appearing to be irregular with many exceptions. However, if you understand the history of the language and how words are constructed, it is 95% regular. It is so predictable that many very young children learn to read without intentional instruction.

- **English uses a foreign alphabet.**

    The Anglo-Saxons, the early English, used *runes* to write. This is what they looked like.

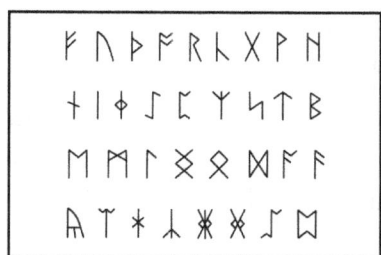

When the Anglo-Saxons met the Romans, they realized how efficient an alphabet could be. So they adopted it.

But there was a major problem. The Roman alphabet did not have enough letters to match all of the sounds in the Anglo-Saxon language. There was a mismatch between the number of letters in the Roman alphabet and the number of speech sounds in the Anglo-Saxon language.

26 letters   42 - 44 speech sounds

To accommodate the extra sounds, letters were combined to spell the extra sounds such as *th* for the sound /th/ and *ng* for the sound /ng/.

- **There are 15 to 16 vowel sounds in English.**

    We teach the five vowels: a, e, i, o, u, and that is a good thing. But don't confuse the number of vowel *letters* with the number of vowel *sounds*. For example, if you are from the northeast states, you may use 16 vowel sounds because you pronounce the short /ŏ/ as in *cot* differently than the /au/ as in *daughter*.

    If you live in other states, you may pronounce the short /ŏ/ and /au/ exactly the same way and so are using only 15 vowel sounds. There are also other variations in pronunciation of vowels and consonants throughout the states.

The Sixteen Vowel Sounds of English

Short Vowel Sounds					
/ă/	/ĕ/	/ĭ/	/ŏ/	/ŭ/	/oo/
Long Vowel Sounds					
/ā/	/ē/	/ī/	/ō/	/ū/	/oo/
Other Vowel Sounds					
/au/	/oi/	/ou/	/ar/		

- **Y is usually a vowel.**

    We say the vowels are "a, e, i, o, u, and sometimes y." But *y* is usually a vowel sound, either independently or in combination with another vowel. It is rarely a consonant.

/ā/	/ē/	/ī/	/oi/
_ay	_y _ey	_y	_oy

- **English words are pulled from three different language groups.**

  The basic structure and everyday words are Anglo-Saxon but only 20% of our words come from that language group. Over 60% of the words come from Latin (and French), and about 18% come from Greek.

Anglo-Saxon 20%	Latin (French) 60%	Greek 18%

This is the reason for so many different spellings for the same sound. For example for the speech sound /sh/, we have five spellings with *ti* being the most common way to spell /sh/ as in the words *nation*, *station*, and *institution*.

Ways to spell the speech sound /sh/			
Anglo-Saxon	Latin	French	Greek
sh as in show	*ti* as in *nation* *si* as in *mission*	*ch* as in *chauffeur*	*ci* as in *musician*

Teaching the alphabet

The letters of the alphabet are the building blocks of all graphemes and all words. Students need to know both the name of the letters and the sounds they represent. Here are guidelines for teaching students who do not know the alphabet.

1. **Start with the speech sound**

   If we use the same sequence the brain uses in processing words, we start with the speech sound. Say the sound and then introduce the grapheme that represents the sound.

   "Today we will learn how to spell the sound /g/."

   Notice how this differs from the traditional approach which starts with the letter and the "sound" it makes.

Brain-based Sequence	Traditional Sequence	
Starts with speech sound	**Starts with letter**	
"Today we will learn how to spell the sound /g/." g	"What sound does the letter g make?" /g/	"What are all the sounds the letter g can make?" /g/ and /j/

2. **Show how to write the grapheme.**

   Say the sound and demonstrate how to properly form both the small and capital letters. Use penmanship lines so students know how to make the letter properly. Talk through the process as you show them how to form the letters. A more detailed description on how to teach handwriting is found later in this chapter.

   Teach the letter name. Researchers have found that children learn the sounds more readily when they know letter names than when they do not. It also makes communication about letters easier. How would you refer to an object if it had no label?

   Have children write the lowercase letter in the air three times while saying the sound. They should use full arm movements as they copy you. Be sure to face the same direction as your students so they can see how to "write" the letter.

   Have children write 3 - 5 small and capitals letters on penmanship paper. Have them look at their work and put a small X above the small and capital letter they think they formed the best.

3. **Feel how the sound is produced in the mouth**

   Have students observe how the sound is formed in the mouth and throat with the tongue and lips.

   "Where is your tongue? What shape is your mouth?"

   This is not meant to be a scientific description of the formation of a sound. The purpose is to increase awareness of the physical differences in producing each sound. This helps many students learn how to differentiate the sounds.

4. **Act out the sound.**

   Acting out the sound is one of the most powerful strategies you can use. For some students, this activity alone makes the difference between reading failure and reading success. Students act out the speech sound that an object or action ***makes***. This creates a mental picture of the speech sound, a mental picture that connects the grapheme with the sound it represents. Some students are not able to make the connection between the speech sound and the grapheme without this kinesthetic activity.

   For example, for the speech sound /sh/, students put their finger to their mouths and say /sh/, /sh/, /sh/. This kinesthetic motion creates a mental picture of telling someone to be quiet. Students are shown the grapheme *sh* as they do the motion so the connection is established between the speech sound and the grapheme that represents it.

   This strategy helps students who are unable to learn letters and the speech sounds they represent in any other way. Once students have learned a sound, review all of the sounds learned so far by showing flash cards of the graphemes while having them act out the sound. A list of suggested motions for all the graphemes are found in Appendix B.

   Acting out something that ***makes*** the sound differs significantly from acting out a word that ***begins*** with the sound. Students who need the actions most are unable to identify the initial sound of a word. For example, "h is for "hat" means nothing to students who cannot segment that initial /h/ sound in the word hat. If they make the motion to represent putting on a hat, the brain makes no connection between the speech sound and the letter representation. Over the years working as a reading specialist, I would see students who were able to make all the motions and say the sounds, but they could not read. In contrast, if students pretend they are out of breath running and saying, "/h/.../h/," they are performing a motion that actually makes that sound.

NOT begins with /h/	BUT makes the sound /h/

Acting out the sound is one of the most powerful strategies you can use.
It can make the difference between learning to read and not learning to read.

Temica was entering 2nd grade, but the specialists told her teacher, "Don't be overly concerned about the progress Temica is making. *She is not capable of learning her letters and sounds.*"

And so she entered second grade below kindergarten level, not even knowing the letters of the alphabet or the sounds they represented. However, the teacher and others working with Temica began implementing the principles found in this book, including acting out the sound. And she made progress.

Just eight months later in April, I visited Temica and taught her a lesson. She was not only reading at grade level, but rapidly and accurately spelling words such as *place, wage, huge*, and *budge* and adding prefixes and suffixes to those words. When principles and practices were used that fit her needs and learning style, she learned to read.

5. **Practice all the ways to know the alphabet.**

   What does it mean to "know the alphabet?" It requires more than just identifying letters and sounds. Students should be able to do each of the following.

When given the NAME of a letter	When given the SOUND	When SHOWN a letter
write it	write the letter	say the name
find it	find the letter	say the sound
say the sound	name the letter	

These skills may seem nearly the same, but they are quite different from each other. A student can do one but not the other. In the first weeks of kindergarten, children may have some difficulty writing letters. You can use lower case letter tiles or magnetic letters instead. In addition to these skills, students should be able to say the alphabet, and by the end of second grade, know how to alphabetize to the third letter.

6. **Use cards, tiles, and manipulatives.**

   Struggling students must use their large muscles to learn so letter cards, letter tiles, or letter blocks are essential. They need them to respond while playing alphabet games. Ask students to find the letter when you say the *name* of the letter or when you say the *speech sound*. You can also use a full game board when students know most of the letters.

a	b	c	d	e
f	g	h	i	j
k	l	m	n	o
p	q	e	s	t
u	v	w	x	y
z				

   Alphabet Show Me Game

   Students match letter tiles to the letter on the game board before starting the game. Then ask students to find the letter when you say the name of the letter or say the speech sound.

   "Show me. . . ."

   Sometimes students also need cards or tiles to express what they already know. Mia was in first grade but could not say her alphabet in order. I gave her letters tiles and asked her to put them in order. She laid them out in perfect alphabetic order. Then she took the next step of saying the letters in the order in which she placed them.

   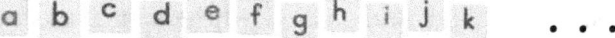

7. **Use only the graphemes the student knows plus one.**

   When I came into the resource room in November, Kyle was a first grade student who did not know any of his letters and sounds. When I tested him, sure enough, he didn't know a single letter. I gave him a letter card to hold and manipulate and introduced the sound and letter name. We found objects that began with that sound. I then gave him a second letter card. We played games with the two cards where he had to show me either the letter that represented a particular sound or the name of the letter. As he gained skill with the two letters, I introduced one more letter. I continued in the same manner, and within three days, he knew eight letters. The kinesthetic component was what he needed to learn the letters and sounds. He manipulated the cards.

Once a student knows two letters you can begin phonemic awareness games with the cards. Keep in mind that oral phonemic awareness games are *not* beneficial to kinesthetic learners.

8. **Don't teach confusing letters together.**

   Some letters are visually similar which makes it difficult for some students to distinguish them. Teach the letters in these pairs at least two weeks apart. This gives students time to learn the one letter before introducing the other letter.

       b and d   p and q   m and n   w and v

Writing the letters

Researchers have found that writing the letters helps students remember the names of the letters as well as the speech sounds they represent. Poor readers, though, may have several types of issues when writing letters.

- **Show students how to hold a pencil properly.**

- **Give verbal clues so letters face the correct way.**

  Kinesthetic learners may not know how to place a letter they see in three dimensions in their mind on a two-dimensional piece of paper. They can turn the letter *b* in any position in their head. If you just pivot the *b*, it becomes a *d*. If you flip the *b*, it becomes *q*. Or if you pivot it and then flip it, it becomes a *p*. So if you see them write a *d*, *q*, or *p* instead of a *b*, it most likely does *not* mean they don't know what a *b* is or what sound it represents. They just don't know how to put it on paper.

  Provide verbal clues that remind students how it looks. For example, *"the capital B and the small b face the same way."* If they write the letter *s, c,* or any other letter backwards, just let them know the letter is *"facing the wrong way"* and have them correct it. Just quietly give a reminder statement and have them correct the reversed letter. They might need many reminders before it becomes habit to form the letters correctly. They soon learn how to write the letters properly.

Give verbal cues that help students know how to write a letter a correctly.

- **Show students how to form letters properly.**

The following guidelines may help you teach students how to form letters as suggested by Ramalda Spalding. Talk through each part of the letter formation.

Line letters

When teaching a line letter, show students how to begin at the top and draw a straight line down. Write the entire letter without lifting the pencil, retracing part of the letter. The following are line letters.

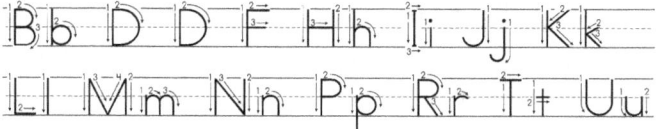

Clock Letters

Clock letters start at 2:00 and go in a curve counterclockwise around the clock. This prevents starting the circle at the bottom or starting at the top but not enclosing the circle. When teaching a clock letter, students need to see a clock with numbers and hands and identify the position to start the clock letters. They need to practice starting at 2:00 by writing in the air. The following are clock letters. All of them start at 2:00.

Letters with Slant Lines

There are a few letters that start with a slant line. These still start at the top, but rather than coming straight down, they slant to the right or to the left.

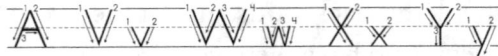

Letters with Horizontal Lines

Two letters have horizontal lines. Teach students how to form these lines straight across.

- **Tracing letters helps students learn the names and sounds they represent.**

  Tracing regular kindergarten-size letters provides the guide students need. For students who have great difficulty remembering the name of letters, tracing five- or six-inch-high letters while standing at a chalkboard or whiteboard may help them. Having the arm cross the mid-section of the body as they trace the letters stimulates the brain. They need to say the name or sounds of the letters as they trace them. They are using the large muscles, a kinesthetic activity which meets their learning style.

  Travis was a special education student who started kindergarten at seven years old. From the time he was four years old, specialists had been working with him to write his name but were unsuccessful. After three weeks of tracing his name in six-inch high letters at the chalkboard, he could spell his name independently.

- *Writing with pen or pencil on paper may be difficult.*

  Some students can write words with perfect spelling on a whiteboard, but find it difficult to write the same words correctly with a pencil. Be aware of this difficulty and provide practice doing both. If students write words or sentences on a whiteboard, they need to also write them on paper. Use the principles of errorless learning and immediate feedback so students can correct their errors. Remember how I guided Drew (Chapter Three) in writing on the chalkboard and then on paper.

Teaching graphemes beyond the alphabet

Students in Grades 2 and up, even poor readers, usually know the alphabet, but many do not know all of the graphemes beyond the alphabet. The ten vowel spellings beyond the short vowels and some of the consonant combinations such as *tch*, *ng*, and *dge* are usually problematic for them. Here are the important graphemes beyond the alphabet that students need to know.

Graphemes beyond the alphabet

ā	ē	ī	ō	ū	oo
a_e	e_e	i_e	o_e	u_e	u_e
ai	ee	igh	oa	_ue	_ue
ay	ea	_ie	ow	_ew	u
eigh	y	y			ui
					ew
oi	au	ou	ar	c	f
oy	aw	ow		k	ph
	a			ck	gh
				ch	
j	m	n	r	s	th
g(e)	mb	kn	er	c(e)	(thin)
g(i)		gn	ir	c(i)	
g(y)			ur	c(y_)	
			ear		
			wr		
th	sh	ch	wh	_ng	_s_
(the)	ti	tch		_n_	
	si				
	ci				

Teach these graphemes using similar guidelines for teaching the alphabet.

- **Start with the speech sound.**

    Introduce the ways to spell a single sound and the principles that govern how they are used. Some spellings only occur in the beginning or middle while others only occur at the end. You will find these principles in Appendix C.

    > - "Today we are going to learn two ways to spell the sound /oi/. The spelling *oi* is found at the beginning and middle of words; *oy* is usually used at the end."

- **Use cards.**

    Use cards for these graphemes when playing the phonemic awareness games so students associate the sound with the various spellings of the graphemes.

- **Don't teach confusing graphemes together.**

    You can usually teach all of the spellings of a sound at the same time. The exceptions are the *er, ir, ur* spellings of /r/ and the *ti, ci, si* spellings of /sh/. These graphemes have no strict rules to govern which spelling to use so they can be confusing. It is best to teach the graphemes for each of these sounds separated by at least two or three lessons.

Letters give only approximations of sounds

Letters and letter combinations only give us an approximation of speech sounds. Some relationships are direct, such as *m* which represents /m/, but others only give us clues to the speech sound. For example, the *augh* grapheme in *caught* and *daughter* is pronounced differently in different parts of the country. We are able to adjust words for our particular accent. This principle also helps us read new words even when the correspondence is remote. Beginning readers with good letter to sound understanding can adjust the word *said* from *sade* to *sed* and the word *there* from *theer* to *thĕr*.

Chapter 8:
The Secret of Markers:
The Missing Content

What you don't know CAN hurt you.

The powerful markers: e, i, y

To truly understand English, you have to understand how the letters *e, i,* and *y* can change words when they are in specific positions. The concept is fairly simple and straightforward and helps us read and spell thousands of words. If you are a good reader, you are already consciously or unconsciously aware of how these letters affect words.

Struggling readers, however, are totally unaware of the markers and what they do. Kinesthetic learners like to see the big picture and to know why. If you teach the following big picture principles in the first four lessons to struggling readers in Grades 2 and up, they will have access to over 8000 words they could never read before.

The markers e, i, and y change the way a letter sounds.

The markers e, i, and y make
1. The vowel long.
2. The c say /s/.
3. The g say /j/.

The following lessons show how to introduce the principle of the markers. NOTE: Children in Grade 1 learn these principles but in a different sequence.

Lesson 1: Markers make the vowel long

When you have the arrangement of *vowel – consonant - marker*, the vowel says its name. You see this arrangement in simple words such as *like* and *made*, and in more complex words such as *computer* where the e makes the *u* long.

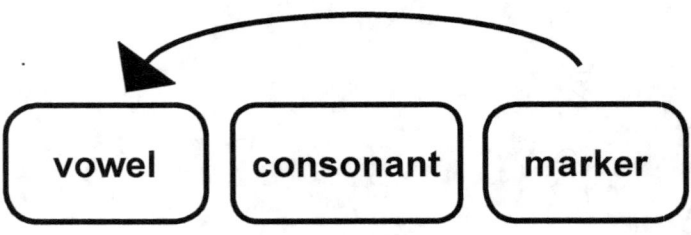

It does not matter where the marker occurs in the word. The rule operates everywhere in our language.

1. **In the middle of a word:** institution, bicycle
   The *i* is making the *u* say /oo/; the *y* is make the *i* say /ī/.

2. **At the end of a word:** like, baby
   The *e* is making the *i* say /ī/; the *y* is make the *a* say /ā/.

3. **In a suffix:** making, exploding
   The *i* is making the *a* say /ā/; the *i* is make the *o* say /ō/.

Exceptions

Although markers work in a remarkably consistent way, you will find exceptions. Sometimes, there is no recognizable reason for the exception, such as in the words *cabinet* or *coliseum*. Markers usually do not work on unstressed syllables in multisyllable words. The word *opening* is an example.

opening

In *opening*, the marker *e* makes the *o* long but the marker *i* is not making the *e* long. The *e* is in an unstressed syllable.

Adding suffixes

If a word **ends** in a marker and the suffix **begins** with a marker, ***you throw away the extra marker.***

mak*e* + ing = making   lik*e* + ed + ed

Traditional phonics uses the *"magic e" or the "silent e"* to touch on this concept, but it is misleading. The letter *e* is not the only letter that makes the vowel long; letters *i* and y do the same thing. In addition, the letter *e* is not always silent, and it can come in the middle of a word, not just at the end. Rather than address only one marker and one task of the marker, it is best to give the full story of all three tasks of all three markers.

Lesson 2: Stopping the marker

We do not always want long vowels so how do we stop the markers from working? We have to be careful when adding suffixes that begin with a marker such as *ed*, *ing*, and *es*. We have to stop those markers from working if we want the vowel to have a short sound. How do we do that? Any two consonants between the vowel and the marker will stop it from working. ***It can be two different consonants or two consonants that are alike.***

The marker is working.

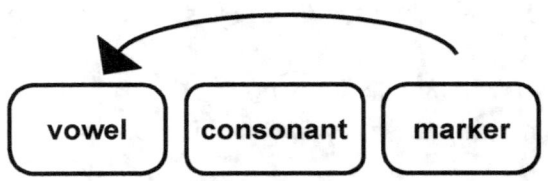

Stop the marker with two consonants.

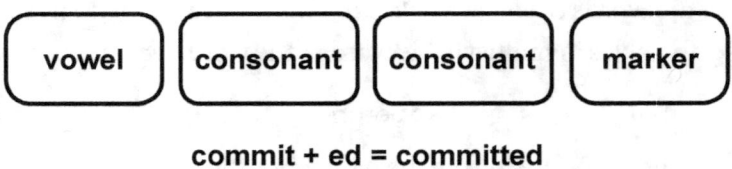

commit + ed = committed

commit + ment = commitment

- In the word *commit*, there are two *m's* that prevent the marker *i* from making the vowel *o* long.
- When adding the suffix *ed*, we had to double the *t* to stop the marker from making the vowel *i* long since it is a stressed syllable.
- The suffix *ment* starts with a consonant so the *t* and *m* stop the marker.

The Skinny L

Sometimes two consonants are not enough. In words ending in _le such as in the word *table*, the vowel is still long. Although the *l* is one of the two consonants between the vowel and the marker, **the l is so skinny it does not stop the marker from working.** You still need to double the consonant.

title   stable   little   middle

In the word *title* and *stable*, the marker *e* makes the vowel long because the *l* is too skinny to stop it. In the word *little* and *middle*, we double the consonant so the marker *e* is stopped.

Lesson 3: The markers make the c say /s/

When a marker *immediately follows* the letter *c*, it will make the *c* say /s/. It is written *ce, ci,* or *cy*. The one exception is the word *Celtic* which can be pronounced either with the /k/ or the /s/ sound. *Celtic* is a proper name and names often break the rules.

ice   icy   icing

Notice the markers *e, i,* and *y* not only make the *c* say /s/ but also make the vowel long.

Here are some examples of words where the markers make the c say /s/. Some of the words also have markers that make the vowel long. Notice in the words *accelerate, accent,* and *accident,* the first *c* says /k/ and the second *c* says /s/. Also, notice that the marker does not work on unstressed syllables.

re**ce**de	**ci**nch	**cy**clone
ac**ce**lerate	ac**ci**dent	conspira**cy**
ac**ce**nt	**ci**vilization	en**cy**clopedia

The sound /k/ at the <u>beginning</u> of a word

There are three common spellings of /k/ with predictable positions in words.

- *c* is usually used at the beginning of a word.
- *k* is usually used in the middle and at the end of a word.
- *ck* is used after a short vowel. The exception is *yak*.

If the letter *c* is followed by a marker, the *c* says /s/. If we want the /k/ sound at the beginning, we are forced to use a *k* as in the words *kitchen, kilt,* and *kind*. If we used the *c*, we have a problem because the marker would cause us to pronounce the words *sitchen, silt,* and *sind*.

kitten	kettle	kelp
kick	kidnap	kite
kindle	keyboard	kindergarten

The sound /k/ after a short vowel

We use the spelling *ck* after a short vowel for two reasons:

1. *The ck stops the marker from making the vowel long.* When we add endings like *_ed* or *_ing*, the two consonants *ck* stop the marker from making the vowel long as in the words *packed* and *licking*.

2. *The ck also stops the marker from making the c say /s/.* If we did not have the extra *k*, the marker in the endings like *_ed* or *_ing* would make the *c* say /s/. Without the *k*, the word *packing* would be *pacing*. The vowel would be long and the *c* would say /s/.

Words that end in *ck* are "marker ready" but we have to add the *k* to make *ck* in some words. For example, we have to add a *k* to *picnic* before adding the suffix *_ing* or *_ed*. We do not want the *i* long or the *c* saying /s/.

picnic + ing is *not* picnicing

but picni<u>ck</u>ing

"Marker ready" _ck	Add a k
shocking	mimic + k = mim**ick**ing
tricky	frolic + k = froli**ck**ing
packed	traffic + k = trafficking

Lesson 4: The markers make the g say /j/

A marker right after the letter *g* will usually make the *g* say /j/ as in *giant*, *aging*, and *gym*. A few common words that are the exception are *give*, *gift*, and *get*. You will also see a few additional exceptions with this spelling.

age

In the word *age*, the marker *e* is making the *g* say /j/ and the vowel *a* long.

Stopping the marker with _dge

We usually stop the marker from working by doubling the consonant, but this is a problem with the *g* that says /j/. If we want to write the word *badge*, we want a short vowel, but also want the *ge* to say /j/.

The problem: If we double the g, the first g will say /g/ because it has no marker and the second g will say /j/. So we have the word *bagge* = bag - j.

bagge

Instead, we add a *d* rather than doubling the *g*. The two consonants *d* and *g* stop the marker from making the vowel long but still allows the marker to make the g say /j/. The letter *d* is not pronounced. Its *only* task is to stop the marker.

badge

Here are some words that use the _dge spelling of /j/.

judge	knowledge	cartridge	dislodge
fidget	acknowledge	porridge	budget
partridge	gadget	smudge	bludgeon

The letter v and markers

The letter v has distinct characteristics that affects how markers work.

- ***It never comes at the end of an English word.*** That means there is usually an *e* after it.

- ***It is never doubled*** (except for the word *savvy*). That means you will have the *vowel-consonant-marker* configuration.

- ***It can stop a marker all by itself.*** Since it is never doubled, you don't know if the vowel is long or short in words such as *gave, have,* and *give*. Is it lĭve or līve? I tell students to try the word both ways.

In Summary

The markers *e, i,* and *y* do the following three things.

1. ***Change the sound a letter makes.***
    - Makes the vowel long
    - Makes the *c* say /s/
    - Makes the *g* say /j/

2. ***Change the way you add endings to words.***
   - Double the consonant to stop the marker.
   - Throw away the extra marker if the suffix begins with a marker.

3. ***Change what graphemes you need to use.***
   - Use _dge to stop the marker.
   - Use a *k* at the beginning of a word instead of *c* when it is followed by a marker.
   - Use _ck to stop the marker.

Chapter 9:
The Secret to Building Words

**Students learn to read by spelling.
They learn to spell by writing.**

Hearing the individual sounds in words and knowing the way to spell these sounds are the foundational skills in learning to read. Using these two skills, the brain "constructs" the word including any prefixes and suffixes.

The Right Instruction	<ul><li>Errorless learning and immediate feedback</li><li>Confidence that students can achieve</li><li>Kinesthetic strategies for every concept.</li></ul>
The Right Content	<ul><li>Hear the individual sounds in spoken words</li><li>Know the spellings of the 42-44 speech sounds</li><li>**Put sounds and spellings together to form words**</li><li>**Know how to add prefixes and suffixes**</li><li>Be able to decode small and big words</li><li>Read smoothly with expression</li><li>Think about meaning</li></ul>
The Right Sequence	<ul><li>The sequence the brain uses in processing words</li></ul>

Spelling before reading

After identifying the speech sound and connecting it to the grapheme, the brain builds the word piece by piece. It is "spelling" the word before reading the word. If we teach reading in the same order that the brain processes words, the natural next step is to build words using the knowledge of phonemes and graphemes.

How we teach students to read matters. It can make the difference between success and failure in reading for many students. Using the same sequence the brain uses produces extraordinary results with both beginning readers and struggling readers.

Look at the chart. Notice how both the skills and the sequence of brain-based reading instruction differs significantly from the two traditional approaches to teaching reading. Traditional approaches start with print rather than the speech sound. No connection is usually made between the speech sound and the letter representations. Even if these programs teach phonemic awareness, it is usually taught in isolation without regard to the sequence the brain uses in processing words.

Brain-based Instruction	Traditional Phonics	Sight word-Phonics
speech sound ↓ spelling of sound ↓ build words ↓ decode and read	letters ↓ sounds of letters ↓ decode and read	letters ↓ sounds of letters ↓ sight words ↓ read

Scientific research has demonstrated that teaching reading in the same sequence that the brain "reads" is the key to helping *all* students learn to read well. ***That means spelling words before reading them.*** Despite the confirmation from research that it is easier for students to learn to read by spelling words *before* reading them, this has not been implemented in most classrooms.

> *"The fundamental flaw found in almost all phonics programs, including traditional ones, is that they **teach the code backwards.** That is, they go from **letter to sound** instead of from **sound to letter**....The print-to-sound approach (conventional phonics) leaves gaps, invites confusion, and creates inefficiencies."*
>
> *--Louisa Moats*
> *Teaching Decoding, American Educator, 1998*

Young preschool children who learn to read without deliberate instruction, use this sequence. They know their letters and hear the speech sounds. Then they spell words *before* they can read. The process of spelling words gives them the foundation for becoming very good readers.

Struggling readers, especially those who are in the upper grades, usually hate to read and the thought brings great anxiety. If we use the right instruction to teach the right content in the right sequence they can become proficient readers. This is more effective than merely supporting reading comprehension through various reading strategies. So how do we teach them how to become skilled readers?

- Have students *spell words on a whiteboard before reading them*. It removes the threat of having to read and engages them in a kinesthetic activity.

- Use the principles of errorless learning and immediate feedback, guiding students to spell every word correctly so they feel the success.

Guidelines for word building

1. **Students will spell words before ever reading them.**

    We want to use the same sequence the brain uses in processing words. *That means students will spell words before they ever read them.* Even very young children find it easier to spell (encode) than to read (decode) the words.

2. **Students must write on a whiteboard or iPad.**

    DO NOT use pencil and paper. Students who struggle the most with reading are often kinesthetic learners and will not do well writing the words on paper. Writing on the whiteboard is a kinesthetic activity that uses the large muscles. Standing is best but not required. The whiteboard has another advantage. When students write on the whiteboard, either standing or sitting, the arm usually crosses the mid-body, which stimulates both sides of the brain to communicate with one another.

    If students use an iPad make sure the program requires the use of the full arm and allows them to easily correct errors.

3. **Introduce one or more ways to spell a sound.**

    Introduce one or more ways to spell a sound. Give the principle that governs those spellings. In spite of the foreign alphabet and the foreign influence on words, English is very consistent and governed by very strict principles. The "Real Rules" of English, found in Appendix C, explain the principles that guide the construction of words.

4. **Limit "teacher talk."**

    Many students, especially kinesthetic learners, do not learn well by seeing or listening. Long explanations with examples do not help them much. Be very brief. Even the introductory instruction should be in the form of questions so if students know the answer, they can respond. If not, tell them. This direct instruction takes only 1 to 5 minutes.

> **Introduce the speech sound /ou/**
>
> - "How do you spell the sound /ou/?"
>   *Teacher writes ou and ow.*
> - "ou is the middle spelling of /ou/."
>   *Teacher writes the word cloud.*
> - "What is the word?"
> - "ow is the end spelling of /ou/."
>   *Teacher writes the word cow.*
> - "What is the word?"
> - "We use ow in the middle if the word ends in l or n."
>   *Teacher writes the words owl and brown.*
> - "What are the words?"
> - "Notice the l and n at the end. Why did we use the ow spelling?"

5. **Choose words with the graphemes you just introduced.**

   Choose words that use the graphemes you have just introduced and that are familiar to the students. Don't choose "baby words" like *mat* or *rat* unless you are teaching students in kindergarten and early first grade. Choose words that are appropriate for the grade level of the student and yet are not too difficult for them to spell when you give a little help. Here is an example of possible words for the sound /ou/.

town	shower	pound	count
scowl	power	found	amount
encounter	profound	scrounge	surround

6. **Use only the graphemes you have taught.**

   This is trickier than you might think. It is easy to unknowingly slip in a word that has graphemes you have not taught.

7. **Choose words that require your help.**

   Choose words with the right level of difficulty.

   - *Too easy.* Students can spell the words without any help from you.
   - *Too difficult.* Students need help with every single letter of the word.
   - *Just right.* Students need some help from you to spell the words correctly. They cannot do it alone.

   ---
   *The most significant progress in learning occurs
   when students perform at a level
   that requires some help from you, the teacher.*

   Word building is not a test of what students know. You are not expecting students to know how to spell these words they have never read. Instead, it is an activity where **students learn how to listen for sounds, choose the correct graphemes, and construct words with your help.**

8. **Anticipate and prevent errors.**

   Don't wait until students write the word incorrectly to give help. Imagine a three-year old child asking you to help them write a word. Give the same kind of support to the students you are teaching. Ask questions, provide clues, and even give correct answers if necessary.

   ---
   *Give students all the help they need
   to write the word correctly.*

   Students can do so much more than you think they can. Push them a little. With your help they write the words perfectly.

   - "Write the word *frown.* Listen carefully to the beginning sounds. What do you hear?"
   - You are anticipating students may not hear the /r/ right after /f/.
   - "What spelling of /ou/ will you use? Why?"

If you use words with similar spellings, students begin applying the correct spelling with less and less help. For example, you may want to use the words *power, tower,* and *shower.* By the time students spell *shower* they need less help than when they spelled *power.*

9. **Ask questions to reinforce the principles.**

   In addition to questions that focus on the spellings of the sounds, also ask questions that help students think of the broad principles that govern the graphemes. Notice in the example the questions were asked about *why* the particular spelling was used. Remember, kinesthetic learners love to know why.

10. **Add prefixes and suffixes to the base word.**

    The brain constructs words by making the connection between the speech sounds and the letters that represent them. Part of that construction is adding the prefixes and suffixes to words so they can be stored in the Word Center of the brain. Prefixes and suffixes are taught as part of constructing words. This is in contrast to the traditional approach where a single prefix or suffix is added to several unrelated words as a separate activity after students know how to read the words.

Brain-based Approach		Traditional Approach	
Prefixes and suffixes are added to a single word.		One prefix or suffix is added to unrelated words.	
place	replacing	retie	rebuild
replace	misplaced	rewind	rewrite
replacement	displacement	replace	retell

Introduce specific prefixes and suffixes just at the moment they are needed.

- *First, say the base word.* Have students write the word.

- *Then have them add the prefix or suffix.* Talk about how to spell it. You usually have to tell students how to spell the prefix or suffix the first time it is used.

- *Have students write the word again* if you are having them add a different prefix or suffix.

> - "Write the word *count*. Which spelling of /ou/ will you use? Why?
> - "Now change *count* to *discount*. "What will you add at the beginning? How do you spell it? You just add it without doing anything to *count*. What does the new word mean?
> - "Write the word *count* again. Change it to *counter*. What will you add at the end? How do you spell it?"
> - "Write the word *count* again. Change it to *countless*. What will you add to the end? How do you spell it? What does the word mean?"

11. Add several prefixes and suffixes to the same word.

Take a word and add as many prefixes and suffixes as possible. Usually use words that students already know, although it is an opportunity to introduce new vocabulary. Here are some examples of words that are constructed from base words. You should use only the words appropriate for the age of your students. As you see, knowing a base word and a few prefixes and suffixes significantly increases both word recognition and vocabulary. As students add prefixes and suffixes to words, they begin to recognize them in words that they read.

> frown, frowned, frowning
> power, powerful, powerfully, empower, empowered
> count, counted, counter, encounter, countless, discount
>   counteract, recount, account, accountant, accountable,
>   counterpart

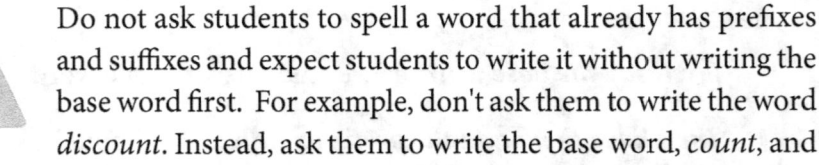

Do not ask students to spell a word that already has prefixes and suffixes and expect students to write it without writing the base word first. For example, don't ask them to write the word *discount*. Instead, ask them to write the base word, *count*, and then ask them to change it to *discount*. Students will be adding a prefix. If you are asking students to write other words formed from *count*, ask them to write the base word again and then add the suffixes or prefixes.

What you need to know about words

Since the words in English come from three main language groups: Anglo-Saxon, Latin (French), and Greek, it makes sense that new words are formed in different ways in these languages. When guiding students in word building, it is helpful to be aware of the differences so you can guide students in forming new words.

How Words Are Formed

Anglo-Saxon	Latin (French)	Greek
Combine two words	prefix + root root + suffix	Combine two roots
sidewalk sunlight	de + plete = deplete com + plete + ion = completion	tri + pod = tripod bio + graph + y = biography

Anglo-Saxon words. New Anglo-Saxon words are formed by combining two words without making any changes to either word. We call these *compound words* and teach them to students in grades K-3. We have hundreds of words that have been formed in this way. For example, the word *walk* is part of over 50 words. Examples are *sidewalk, walkway, walkout,* and *crosswalk.*

Latin words. All Latin words are formed by adding a Latin prefix or suffix to a Latin root. These prefixes, suffixes, and word roots cannot stand alone. An example is the Latin root *mot* that means "move." When prefixes and suffixes are added to this root, we have words like *motion, emotion, motivate, motivation, motor,* and *motel.* Most words from Latin roots are words read in Grades 4 and above.

Greek words. Greek words are formed by adding two roots together. Neither root can stand alone. Children in grades K - 3 can learn some of these roots such as *bi* which means *two* and *graph* which means *write.* They can learn that *triangle* means "three angles" and that *bicycle* means "two circles."

Many of our technical words come from Greek origin such as the words *astrophysics, aquamarine,* and *psychology.* It is helpful for students to understand the meaning of the word roots when they are leaning these words in science and history.

- "You will write words with the Latin root *pose* which means put or place."
  Write pose for students to see.
- "There are over 150 words with this Latin root.
- "On your whiteboard, write the word *pose*. What does it mean?
- "Change it to *position*. What will you do with the marker? You will add the connecting letter *i* and then add *tion*."
- "Write the root pose again Change it to *compose*. The prefix *com* means 'together or with.' What does the new word mean?
- "Now change it to *composer*. What will you add? What does it mean?"

Chapter 10: The Secret to Decoding Words

Take away the fear of words.

This is an amazing fact. Students can hear a word, listen to the sounds, and spell the word perfectly, but then they can't read the word they have just spelled. When you work with students, you will observe how easily they can build words with their knowledge of phonemes and graphemes, but then have no idea how to read those words. It brings home the fact that decoding is a very different skill than spelling or phonemic awareness and must be taught.

The Right Instruction	<ul><li>Errorless learning and immediate feedback</li><li>Confidence that students can achieve</li><li>Kinesthetic strategies for every concept.</li></ul>
The Right Content	<ul><li>Hear the individual sounds in spoken words</li><li>Know the spellings of the 42-44 speech sounds</li><li>Put sounds and spellings together to form words</li><li>Know how to add prefixes and suffixes</li><li>**Be able to decode small and big words**</li><li>Read smoothly with expression</li><li>Think about meaning</li></ul>
The Right Sequence	<ul><li>The sequence the brain uses in processing words</li></ul>

What is decoding?

Decoding is the ability to look at a word, break it apart, attach a sound to each grapheme, and then smoothly blend those sounds together. You decode in exactly the same way the brain processes words. We often call it "sounding out a word."

It is essential that students be taught how to look at words and decode them. If they aren't taught, they are left with two options and neither one uses the languages centers of the left brain.

1. Memorizing the word
2. Guessing the word

Decoding simple words

Students in Kindergarten - Grade 1 who struggle with reading will need to be taught how to decode simple words. Usually, students in Grades 2 and up can read these words. It is the "big" words that scare them.

Students must be taught how to decode.

How do you teach decoding? The natural instinct is to say each individual sound and then try to put the sounds together *fast* to form the word. This is too difficult. Instead, you blend the sounds together by chunks.

1. You say the first sound and then add the next sound.
2. With those sounds together, you add the next sound.
3. You continue doing this until the word is completely blended.

Here is an example. The word is thick.

- Say the first sound . . . . /th/
- Say the second sound . . . . /i/
- Say the two sounds together . . . . /th/ + /i/ = /thi/
- Say the next sound . . . . /k/
- Say the first two sounds and then add the last sound . . . . /thi/ + /k/ = /thick/

Notice how important it is to recognize that *th* and *ck* represent single sounds. If students do not know this, they cannot decode the word.

Help students say the sounds correctly. If /uh/ is added to consonant sounds such as /buh/ instead of /b/ or /kuh/ instead of /k/, students will not be able to blend the sounds together with that extra /uh/ sound. It is important that these sounds are pronounced correctly.

Common decoding problems

- *Guessing.* The first impulse of students who have not had previous experience in decoding is to "guess" the word. That is the only strategy they know, and it may take time for them to get used to decoding. Remind students that it is faster to decode a word than to guess.

- *Afraid of making a mistake.* Some students are afraid they will make a mistake and so they pull words apart they already know. They do not understand it is okay *not* to say each sound in a word slowly. I tell students that their brains "remember" the words they have already "sounded out." Reading the words aloud *with them* at a reasonable pace helps them build confidence to read words they already know.

Joel had just completed first grade, but was still sounding out every individual sound in a word. It was painful to listen to him read. After assessing him, I found he had all the skills necessary to read well. He was just afraid of making a mistake. I explained to him that once he had sounded out a word his brain remembered it. In order to help him gain confidence, I read with him, reading just ahead of him so he was forced to keep on reading.

- *Forgetting to blend.* Some students may still try to blend the sounds together all at once even after you have shown them how to decode. Remind them to "chunk" the sounds before adding the next sound.

- *Continued difficulty.* A few students have difficulty blending sounds together even though they have phonemic awareness and know how to spell words. These are usually young students who are just beginning to read. The following kinesthetic activity will help them learn how to blend sounds together..

Blending the word "map"

The following pictures guide you through the five steps in blending the word map using this kinesthetic strategy. There are also instructions for blending words with four and five sounds.

/m/	**Step 1:** Touch the shoulder and say the first sound.
/a/	**Step 2:** Touch the elbow and say the second sound.

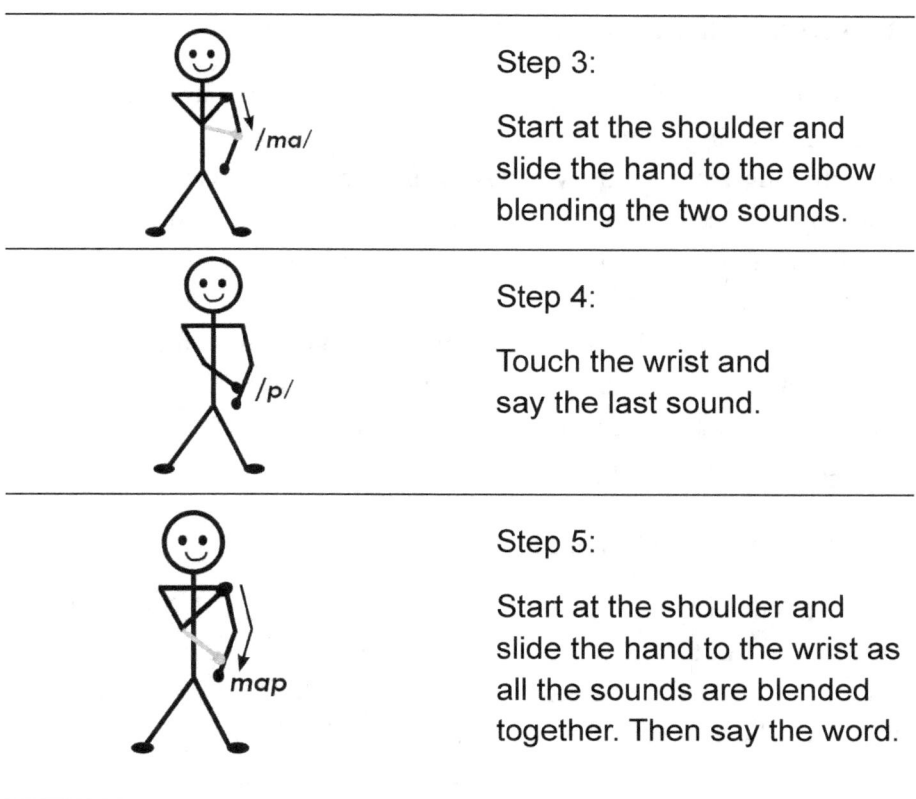

Step 3:	Start at the shoulder and slide the hand to the elbow blending the two sounds.
Step 4:	Touch the wrist and say the last sound.
Step 5:	Start at the shoulder and slide the hand to the wrist as all the sounds are blended together. Then say the word.

A word with four sounds may be decoded like this.

stack

shoulder	s
elbow	t
mid lower arm	a
wrist	ck

A word with five sounds may be decoded like this.

stand

shoulder	s
mid upper arm	t
elbow	a
mid lower arm	n
wrist	d

Vision problems. You may encounter a few students who continue to have decoding issues even after they have phonemic awareness, know the graphemes, and have practiced all of the strategies for decoding. These students with normal intelligence may have issues with their vision such as eye tracking and eye teaming. These types of vision problems will cause continued inability to decode words smoothly. In these cases, a developmental vision specialist can identify and address these problems.

Instant word recognition

A good reader can decode words very rapidly, almost undetectable to someone listening. Once a word has been read several times, the word goes into long-term memory and is automatically retrieved. If it is stored phonologically, it is stored in the Word Center of the brain and will be retrieved instantly. The number of times a word has to be decoded before it is stored there varies with each student. Some can sound out a word only once and remember it. Others must sound out the same word a few times. Watch for insecurity which may cause students to sound out a word more times than needed even though it has already been stored in the brain for instant recognition.

Decoding multisyllable words

Most struggling readers in Grades 2 and up know how to decode and read simple words, but "big" words frighten them. They have no idea how to tackle them. In order to become proficient readers, they need to know how to handle any word they encounter confidently.

Most struggling readers in Grades 2 and up can decode small words, but they cannot decode multisyllable words.

The principle of decoding multisyllable words is the same as decoding simple words except you are looking at *chunks* of the word rather than individual graphemes in the word. Once the word is divided into chunks, then you proceed as with simple words.

1. You say the first chunk and then add the next chunk.
2. With those chunks together, you add the next chunk.
3. You continue doing this until the word is completely blended.

The rules of syllabication cannot be used because they require knowing if the vowels in a word are long or short. Since students can't even read the word, they have no idea if the vowels are long or short. The solution is dividing the word by looking at the consonants.

To divide a word by looking at the consonants, it is absolutely necessary that students "see" graphemes such as *ch, th, tch,* and *ng* as a whole. For this reason, use only words with graphemes that have been introduced. If students recognize the prefixes and suffixes in the word, it helps decoding. However, if students do not recognize them, it will *not* hinder their ability to decode the word.

Here are the guidelines for "chunking" words. Have students take their pencils and practice dividing words before reading them.

> **Where to break apart a word:**
> - Divide <u>before</u> a single consonant.
> - Divide <u>between</u> two consonants.
> - Divide <u>between</u> three consonants in any way you want.
> - Divide a prefix or suffix from the base word if you see one..

How to teach decoding of multisyllable words

- Demonstrate how to break a word into chunks.

- Have students use a pencil or marker to make the slash marks to divide a word into chunks.

- Demonstrate how to read each chunk and put the chunks together. Do two or three words with them.

- Then give them time to chunk a word with a pencil or marker and put the chunks together independently. Provide help when needed.

- In a very short time, students do not need to use their pencils but are able to break a word apart mentally and put it back together.

Continually reinforce the fact that it is faster to break a word apart than to guess. Many students are so used to guessing they will be tempted to do just that. I love it when students say to me, "It IS faster to break the word apart than to guess!"

It is faster to break a word apart than it is to guess.

Here is an example. The word is circumference.

- First break the word apart. . . . . cir|cum|fe|rence OR
    cir|cum|fer|ence

- Say the first chunk . . . . /cir/

- Say the second chunk . . . . /cum/

- Say the two chunks together . . . . . /cir/+/cum/= /circum/

- Say the next chunk . . . . /fer/

- Say the first two chunks and then add the third chunk . . . . /circum/+fer/=/circumfer/

- Say the next chunk . . . . /ence/

- Say the first three chunks and then add the last chunk . . . . /circumfer/+/ence/= circumference

Provide challenge words

For each lesson, provide challenge words for students to decode that are appropriate for their grade level. These are words students have *not* spelled but are words in their listening or grade level reading vocabulary. They have heard these words. This gives them practice, under your guidance, in tackling multisyllable words.

For the words with the *ou/ow* spellings, the following words might be some of the challenging words.

announce	announcement	pronounce	mispronounce
pronunciation	mispronunciation	astounding	surroundings
accountability	miscounted	counterfeit	counteracted

The following is an example on how to teach decoding of multisyllable words.

- "When we come across a word we don't know, we need to break it apart before we try to read it. It is faster to break a word apart than to guess.

    (*The word is accountability.*)

- "First, take your pencil and put slash marks on the word to show where you would break it apart. Divide <u>before</u> a single consonant. Divide <u>between</u> two consonants.

- "Where should we divide this word?

    Guide students in dividing the word into chunks

    . ac | coun | ta | bi | li | ty

- "Now let's put the chunks together. What does ac say?
- Yes. Now what does coun say? Let's put the two sounds together. accoun.
- "What does the next chunk say? ta
- Now put that with the accoun. accounta
- What does the next chunk say? bi
- Put it with the first chunks. accountabi
- (Continue until the word is completely blended. Many times students will know what the word is by the time they have blended most of the chunks.

Pronunciation issues

- **Prefixes and suffixes can change the vowel sound.**

    Pronunciation can get tricky because vowels can change from long to short or from short to long as you add prefixes and suffixes. Tell students to try the vowels both ways. Many of these words are already in their listening vocabulary so they will recognize the word.

    apply . . . **application** *(change in the sound a makes)*
    paralysis . . . **paralyze** *(change in the sound y makes)*
    nation . . . **national** *(change in the sound a makes)*

- **The placement of the stressed syllable can also change the pronunciation.**

  When prefixes and suffixes are added, the placement of the stressed syllable may change, altering the vowel sound. Students need to be aware of this possibility. Remember, markers usually do not work on unstressed syllables.

  In the following examples, notice the difference in the vowel sound when the suffix is added. The suffix has changed the stressed syllable and consequently changed the vowel sound.

  pre**fer** . . . **pref**erence   ex**pire** . . . expir**a**tion

- **The prefix and suffix changes the meaning of the word.**

  Prefixes and suffixes help us know what the word means. The word *nation* names a thing. When we describe a *nation*, we add the suffix *al* and have *national*. The prefix *inter* often means "between or among." Something that is *international* is between many nations. Teach the meaning of the prefixes and suffixes as you introduce them.

- **Sometimes two vowels together make separate sounds.**

  In some words, the two vowels together must be pronounced separately. You may have to just tell students how to pronounce these words.

  cr*ea*te   rad*io*   autob*io*graphy

Don't underestimate students

I taught a lesson to three fifth grade special education students who were reading at a second and third grade level. They had been building words, but only words they could spell almost independently. They also were not reading any challenge words because the words seemed "too difficult."

When I worked with them, I bumped up the difficulty of the words so I had to give them some help in spelling the words. And they could do it perfectly with help. I then showed them how to break apart the challenge words and put the chunks back together. They could read them. They could do so much more with just a little help. The teacher was amazed and very pleased. Don't underestimate what these students can do.

Chapter 11:
The Secret to Developing True Fluency

Fluency is the ability to read "like you speak."

Words that are processed in the language centers of the brain and read repeatedly are stored in the Word Center for instant retrieval. This is the foundation for reading smoothly with expression. Students who have not processed words in the language centers will have difficulty with fluency.

The Right Instruction	• Errorless learning and immediate feedback • Confidence that students can achieve • Kinesthetic strategies for every concept.
The Right Content	• Hear the individual sounds in spoken words • Know the spellings of the 42-44 speech sounds • Put sounds and spellings together to form words • Know how to add prefixes and suffixes • Be able to decode small and big words • **Read smoothly with expression** • Think about meaning
The Right Sequence	• The sequence the brain uses in processing words

What is reading fluency?

Reading fluency is the ability to read aloud smoothly and accurately with appropriate pauses, tone of voice, and expression. Fluent readers read naturally and effortlessly as though they are speaking. Fluency is built upon the foundation of the ability to decode quickly and accurately. The more proficient readers are at decoding, the more likely they will be fluent in their reading.

Good readers are fast readers. The relationship between reading fluency and oral reading rates has led to using oral reading speed as an indicator of fluency. But be careful! Reading fluency is *not* equivalent to reading fast. Having students read a selected text repeatedly or memorize many sight words can shift the focus to reading speed rather than true reading fluency. We can become so anxious to improve reading rate that we may be tempted to skip over the important prerequisites for fluency. When students have all the foundational skills, fluency can be taught, for the most part, in just a few minutes with follow up reminders.

How we really read

To understand reading fluency, we need to know how we read words on a page. We actually do not read word by word. Rather, we see groups of words at one time. The eye moves across a line of text and stops at intermittent points. These punctuated eye movements are called *saccades* (suh-kahds).

We do not read word by word.
We see groups of words at one time.

For example in the sentence "They decided to hike near the lake," you will see the sentence in two or three groups of words. Your eye does not move smoothly from word to word, but stops at a group of words and then quickly moves on to the next group and stops. You may see:

They decided • to hike • near the lake.

Or you may see:

They decided to hike • near the lake.

Your eye span is the number of words you see all at once as you glance at a page. Your eye span can be two to six or seven words. **Even the eye span of a first-grade student is two or three words.** You can actually increase your eye span with practice. Rapid readers can see a whole line or even more in one saccade.

Try it! How many words do you see in a saccade? Find a text and place a folded blank sheet of paper over it. Quickly pull the paper down and then up again to expose a line of text for an instant. How many words did you see?

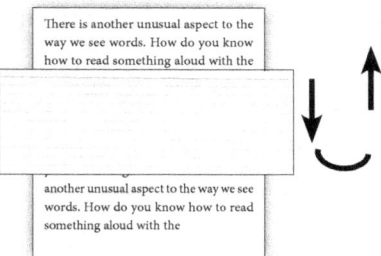

There is another unusual aspect to the way we see words. How do you know how to read something aloud with the right expression before you have even read it? Your brain can process words in the Word Center in nanoseconds. You not only see groups of words, but you also see five to six words *ahead* of what you are reading aloud. Fluent readers, who are reading easy materials, have an eye-voice span of five to six words. In other words, their brains have read the words before they read them aloud. In fact, they are doing two things at once—looking at a set of words while reading aloud another set of words!

Imagine how this could affect the accuracy of reading. We've all done it. We make minor changes to the text as we read aloud. We may reverse words, add words, or substitute words that have the same meaning. It is all part of reading with expression. You are reading aloud virtually from memory so those kinds of errors will occur. These "mistakes" don't change the meaning. This is unlike the types of errors poor readers make. Instead of substituting *car* for *auto*, poor readers will substitute *automatic* for *automobile*. Be sure to distinguish between the two types of errors when listening to your students.

 BE CAREFUL! Since our eyes read groups of words, ***don't allow students to point to each word as they read.*** Pointing at words, word by word, prevents the eye from doing what it wants to do—see groups of words. It will hinder the development of fluency as well as reading speed. If students need help staying on the correct line, have them use a strip of paper or a 3 x 5 card placed under the line of text.

Is it a reading fluency problem?

How will you know if a student has a reading fluency problem, or if it is some other issue that just *looks* like a fluency issue? Poor readers might appear to have issues with fluency or reading comprehension, but the real problem is the lack of phonemic awareness and grapheme knowledge.

What appears to be a fluency issue may not be.

Always go back and assess phonemic awareness and the ability to represent those sounds whenever fluency or comprehension problems surface. When these skills are addressed, decoding and fluency are usually easy to teach.

Assess phonemic awareness and grapheme knowledge to make sure it is a true fluency issue.

The test of a true fluency problem is whether the student can read almost every word of a *new* text without hesitation. The exceptions are beginning readers who are just learning to decode. They may read slowly because they are decoding many words, but they are able to read the words. If the student **cannot** read the words correctly, then it is **not** a fluency issue.

What is the real issue?

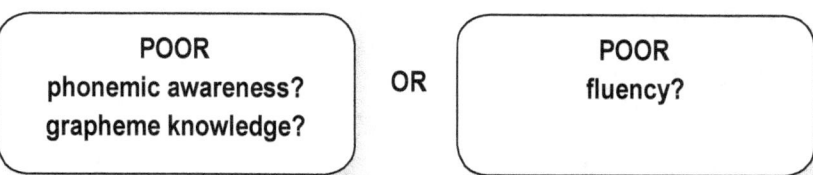

Students who merely have a fluency issue can read all of the words, but may:

- Read word by word OR
- Read without expression OR
- Read right through punctuation as if it were not there.

These students can be taught fluency in a very short time using specific strategies that have been proven to correct the problem.

Teaching fluency

A fluent reader reads smoothly with appropriate pauses, attention to punctuation, and with expression. You will need to explain and model fluency for students who are not fluent.

- **Chunking a sentence**

    Show students as young as the second grade how they actually read words in groups. Ask them to take a 3 x 5 card or a folded piece of paper and cover a line of text. Instruct them to quickly pull it down and up and tell you how many words they see. They can usually see at least two words and often even more. They are usually surprised.

    Explain how our eyes do not read word by word but actually jump from one group of words to another. Show students how to chunk a sentence into phrases according to the number of words they see at a time.

Wes sat • beside his brother.

- **Echo Reading**

    Use echo reading to demonstrate chunking a sentence. Read a sentence, pausing between each chunk so students hear it. Then have students read it back to you using the same expression. It usually takes only a few minutes of instruction and students understand how to chunk. This is not something you will have to continually teach. Just give a few reminders.

- **Voicing Punctuation**

    Punctuation tells us when to pause, when to stop, and what expressions to use. Talk about the intonation of different punctuation. Demonstrate how the voice changes with different punctuation marks.

comma, hyphen, colon, semi-colon	pause
period	stop
questions mark	voice goes up at the end
exclamation mark	excited voice

- **Dramatic reading**

    Read a sentence or two with dramatic expression, and then have students read it back with the same expression. You may have to demonstrate the sentence and have them read it back more than once.

    The following sentence is an example. Talk about the chunks and the punctuation. Then demonstrate to students how to read it dramatically with expression. Then have students practice it aloud together or individually.

    "Wait for me!" cried Anne.

    Teach students how to put on their "acting hat" when they read. As soon as students read their first sentence no matter what their age, they need to be taught how to do this.

- **Choral reading**

    Choral reading is just reading together like a voiced choir. This is a way for students to practice reading in phrases with expression. You can also do choral reading in a very small group to give all students practice reading. Make sure each student actually reads.

- **Reader's Theater**

    Take any passage and have students practice reading parts of it dramatically. One student can read a part, two students can read a part, or a group of students can read a part. It does not have to be a scripted play but any piece that lends itself to dramatic expression or natural divisions such as different people speaking as would be seen in a conversation on a talk show or in a documentary. You can also divide a science or history text into parts, assigning different readers to explain specific information. Be creative!

When fluent readers read aloud, they do so naturally and effortlessly as though they are speaking. Reading is automatic, allowing them to focus attention on the ideas in the text and comprehend the meaning.

decoding   >   fluency   >   comprehension

The more proficient readers are at decoding, the more likely they will be fluent in their reading, and the more likely they will be able to comprehend what they are reading.

In Summary

1. Reading fluency is the ability to read aloud smoothly and accurately with appropriate pauses, tone of voice, and expression. It is *not* equivalent to reading speed.

2. Fluency is built upon the foundation of the ability to decode quickly and accurately.

3. We do not read word by word. We see groups of words at one time.
    - The punctuated eye movements are called *saccades*.
    - Pointing at each word hinders what our eyes want to do -- read groups of words.

4. When we read aloud, we see about five to six words ahead of what we are reading.

5. What appears to be a fluency problem may actually be a lack of foundational skills.
    - Test for phonemic awareness and grapheme knowledge
    - Check decoding skills

6. Strategies for teaching fluency
    - Chunking a sentence
    - Echo reading
    - Voicing punctuation
    - Dramatic reading
    - Choral reading
    - Reader's Theater

Chapter 12: The Secret to Increasing Silent Reading Speed

Silent reading speed significantly impacts the speed of completing school assignments.

Low-performing readers read very slowly with most students reading between 80 and 120 words per minute even after they have become proficient in reading words. They have developed poor habits due to their previous struggle with reading. They usually read word by word and move their lips.

Students who read less than 150 wpm will find it almost impossible to keep up with the reading required in school. Rather than spending four or five hours a night completing homework, many opt not to do it at all. Look at the difference in the amount of time it takes to do the same homework between someone who reads 80 words per minute and one who reads 260 words per minute.

80 wpm   6.25 hrs

260 wpm   2 hrs

That is why silent reading and the silent reading rate must receive our attention. If the reading rate can be doubled, tripled, or even quadrupled, the amount of time it takes to read a text is substantially reduced.

Three types of silent reading

There are three types of reading which places parameters on how fast we can read. Most individuals use the "think-read" method of reading.

1. **Vocalize – 80 - 180 wpm**

    Individuals who move their lips while reading cannot read faster than 150-180 words per minute because that is all the faster we can talk. Most poor readers use this method, articulating every word with their silent, but moving lips. If they are not reading aloud but still moving their lips, it is called *sub-vocalizing*. By forming each word with their lips, these students are not taking advantage of the way they actually see words -- in groups of at least two or three words at a time. By moving their lips, they are slowing down their reading rate when it would not be necessary.

2. **Think-Read – 180 - 400 wpm**

    Most individuals read using this method. Although the lips don't move during reading, every individual word is pronounced in the mind. The average reader reads about 260 words per minute using this method.

3. **Direct Perception – Over 400 wpm**

    With this method, individuals see groups of words and recognize them but do not pronounce them in the mind. They trust that their brains know what it sees. Most of these readers read between 600 – 800 + wpm.

Most people read about 260 words per minute.

Age does not determine which method is used. There are adults who subvocalize and fourth graders who use direct-perception.

Hindrances to silent reading speed

Our goal is to help our students become efficient readers, not to make them speed readers. By the time students reach fifth grade, they should read comfortably between 280 and 400 words per minute with good comprehension. We want them to move from subvocalizing to at least the think–read method of processing words. All of these hindrances can be removed with a small amount of practice.

- **Moving the lips**

    Moving the lips while reading prevents reading faster than 150 wpm. By the time students reach second grade, they need to practice *not* moving their lips while reading. Otherwise, it will become a habit that hinders reading proficiency. Monitor your students and help them overcome this tendency.

- **Reading word by word**

    Reading word by word slows the rate because the reader is pronouncing each word, even though three to seven words may be seen at once. Remember, we do not read word by word. Rather, we see groups of words at one time.

- **Rereading or looking back**

    Backtracking or rereading may be a mark of insecurity or just be a bad habit. Researchers have found that regression can consume up to one-sixth of reading time.

- **Stopping at a word, phrase, or at the end of the line**

  Just pausing to decide where to go next also slows reading speed. Many readers pause at the end of a text line before returning to the next line.

Activities to increase silent reading speed

Grades 2 and 3

The focus of instruction for 2nd and 3rd grade students is only in two areas.

- *How to read in chunks.*

  Have students do Activity #1: Reading in Chunks to help them become aware of how they read in chunks.

- *How to read without moving their lips.*

  Explain the benefits of not moving their lips, and then have them practice reading in that way. Remind them not to move their lips. *Do not* have students do any of the timed readings.

These two strategies alone can dramatically increase their silent reading speed.

Grades 4 and up

Students in these grades will benefit from all of the following activities. Those who are reading at grade level can complete these activities at any time. Struggling readers who are just learning the graphemes need to wait until they have learned most of the graphemes. I teach this to struggling readers in Lesson 40 of 45 lessons.

Activity #1: Reading in chunks

This activity can be done with students as young as first grade to help them read smoothly. This will move them beyond word by word reading.

It is also an activity that is important for all students who have struggled with reading. Most of them are in the habit of reading word by word and are usually surprised at how many words they see. With practice, they can actually increase their eye span.

- Have students get out their books and 3 x 5 cards.

- Students will see at least two or three words at a time. Do this activity two or three times so they understand that they see more than one word. Explain to them how we read in chunks and not word by word.

> - "Open your book to any page and place the 3 x 5 card over a line of words.
> - "When I say 'Go,' jerk the 3 x 5 card down one line and up again in a split second. How many words did you see?"

Activity #2: Base reading speed

Materials Needed

- An easy book with no more than one word per hundred they do not know.

- 3 x 5 card or folded sheet of paper for each student

- Stopwatch or watch with a second hand

- Record sheet for recording reading speed

    Each student should have a copy of a record sheet to record their timings. They will use this sheet to record their timings during class for about three weeks as well as the timings they do at home.

- Have students read for two minutes. Time them.

> - "You will read in your book for two minutes.
> - "I will time you. When I say, 'Go' begin reading and read until I say, 'Stop.' Then mark where you stop."

- Now have students count the number of words they have read. Usually this is best by counting the number of words in a full line and multiplying that by the number lines. The number of words will be close. Then count the individual words in the partial lines. Once a total number of words is determined, have students divide that number by two. That will give the approximate number of words per minute.

- Have students record these numbers on the record sheet.

Sample record sheet for timed readings

	Baseline	Timing #1	Timing #2	Timing #3	Timing #4
# of words in 2 min					
# of words per min					
# of words in 2 min					
# of words per min					

Activity #3: Do not move lips

Not moving the lips or sub-vocalizing will substantially increase silent reading speed. If students are reading at 80 words per minute while moving their lips, they can immediately be reading 150 to 180 words per minute when they stop subvocalizing.

- *Briefly ex*plain the three types of reading students. Let them know that by saying the word, they cannot read faster than they can talk.
- Time students again for two minutes. They are to consciously avoid moving their lips, even if they have to put their hands over their mouth or press their lips together with their fingers.
- Have them record the number of words on the record sheet.
- You may need to repeat this timed activity more than once because some students have entrenched habits of moving their lips. Most students will see a significant increase in silent reading speed with removing this hindrance.

Activity #4: Keep a good pace

Students need to learn to keep a good pace when reading. Students often have a habit of looking back or rereading words and sentences to make sure they have read them correctly. This not only reduces reading speed but also hinders comprehension because it disrupts the flow of the meaning. They need to force themselves to keep reading.

Instruct students to not worry about comprehension but to read as fast as they can. This is important to break the habit of regression. After practicing daily for about three weeks, they can reduce the speed to a comfortable level where comprehension is easy. This reading speed will be three or four times higher than when they first started, and they will understand what they read. Students also must learn to not hesitate at the end of a line, but rapidly return to the next line. When their eyes go to the next line, they need to look at the *second* or *third* word in the line and not the first word. If our eyes return to the first word of a line, part of our sight is on the blank space to the left of the word. It wastes reading time.

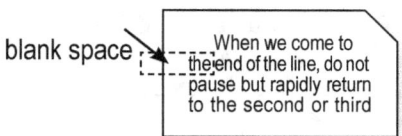

- Demonstrate how to use a 3 x 5 card or folded paper to keep a good pace by placing it just under the line being read. Then keep the card moving down at a rate *faster than is comfortable*. This helps your eyes to keep moving down.

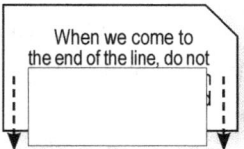

- "Sometimes we get in the habit of rereading words or sentences we have just read to make sure we have read it correctly. But we want to keep reading and not look back. This can be prevented by placing the 3 x 5 card (folded paper) just below the line you are reading.

- "When you come to the end of the line, do not pause. Rapidly return from the end of the line to the **second** word in the next line. If your eyes return to the first word rather than the second word, part of your sight is on a blank to the left of the beginning word and that wastes time.

- "Do not worry about understanding what you are reading. Force yourself to read as fast as you can. This is important to break the habit of pausing or rereading words."

- Time students for two minutes as they implement the strategies they have learned so far. Have them determine the number of words, divide it by two, and record it on the record sheet.

- You may need to repeat this timing activity two or three times in a session to give students the practice they need.

Activity #5: Read the tops of words

- Demonstrate how to read the top of words rather than the bottom of words. Students should also incorporate all of the skills from the previous timed readings.

> - "If you read the tops of words, you can read faster than if your eyes rest on the bottom of the word."

- Time students again for two minutes as they implement all of the strategies. Again, you may need to repeat this timed activity more than once to give students the practice they need.

Owen

Owen was a walking encyclopedia when it came to history, but he could not read well. He was a fifth grader who was reading at the second grade level according to the *Woodcock Reading Mastery Test*. He spent four to five hours every night trying to do his homework. He had hearing problems as a child and a speech impediment that would not improve in spite of three years of speech therapy. He finally concluded that he just had a cool "accent."

After 45 hours of research-based reading instruction that spanned over six months, Owen was reading above grade level and enjoying reading about the history he loved so much. Toward the end of that instruction, he engaged in the activities to increase his reading speed. Although at this point he could read well, he was only reading about 80 words per minute, too slow to function well in school. After three weeks of practice to increase his reading speed, he was reading about 300 words per minute. His greatest delight was being able to finish his homework in less than an hour rather than the former four to five hours.

Activities to increase silent reading speed should be taught only *after* students know most of the graphemes. Also, most of the activities are only appropriate for students in fourth or fifth grade or older. Your goal is not to make them speed readers but to merely increase their reading speed to an average pace for a proficient reader.

Chapter 13:
The Secret of Reading at the
Right Level

**You can't learn to drive without driving
and
you can't learn to read without reading.**

Getting students to read

Students *must* read to become skilled readers. There is no shortcut. We have to particularly address the issue that poor readers have. How do we get students who hate reading and avoid it at all costs to read? How do we do that with the least trauma? We have to make it "doable." They must be successful. Here are the guidelines for all students, including poor readers.

- **In every lesson, begin with non-reading activities.**

    Beginning with non-reading activities removes the immediate dread of reading for those who cannot read well. The three-minute introduction of the graphemes, the phonemic awareness games, and the word building do not require reading but they do provide the tools that help students become successful at reading. If these are taught using errorless learning and kinesthetic strategies, students experience many little successes that boost their confidence and sense of achievement.

- **Have students read the words they have spelled.**

    Students *must* read the words they have just spelled. It has two advantages. First of all, students have just heard every sound in each word and have thought about how it is represented on paper. That gives them confidence to read the words. Secondly, students can't depend on context to "guess" words. Instead, they are forced to use their newfound skills to decode words.

    Provide each student with a copy of the words so they can practice them. If you have a group of students, have one read three or four words, and then have the whole group read them together. Teach students how to decode if necessary. This is an example of some of the words you might use when teaching the graphemes for /ou/.

pound	pounding	proud	proudly
crouch	crouches	count	countdown

- **Have students read challenge words aloud.**

    If students are to become independent readers, they must learn how to tackle any unknown words. If you show them how to divide the challenge words into chunks, they will be able to read them. Every challenge word should have *only* the graphemes you have taught. Here is an example for first grade.

    cabin   raccoon   invite   inside

Here is an example for older students.

    renounce   pronounce   mispronounce
    pronunciation   mispronunciation   astounding
    accountability   counterfeit   counteracted

Most of the words need to be in the listening vocabulary of the students. That means words used for first grade will differ significantly from words used for higher grade levels.

- **Use decodable texts if a student is reading at a beginning first grade level or lower.**

What is a decodable text? A decodable text is one where all the words contain *only* the graphemes students have learned. Why is it important to use decodable texts? If beginning readers are expected to read words with graphemes they have not learned, they develop habits of guessing and become discouraged with reading. They are being asked to read words without the proper tools.

No matter what the age or grade, if a student is reading at a first grade level or lower, use decodable texts. Even a student in 6th grade or 11th grade who reads at first grade level must practice decoding words.

These types of decodable texts may not be easy to find since you want ones that are acceptable for the grade level you are teaching. Also, many texts called "decodable" are not. They may have a few decodable words but they also have many words with sounds students have not learned.

Decodable texts do not have to be boring. Here is the beginning of a decodable story for the first half of first grade that can be used for students of all ages that read at this level. Students have been taught every grapheme in this story.

> A little ant came to the river to get a drink. As she drank, she slipped into the river. She began to sink.
>
> "Save me! Save me!" she cried. "I'm sinking!"
>
> A kind dove was sitting nearby on the branch of a tree. The dove slid a loose branch into the river. The ant grabbed the branch and floated safely to the shore. Soon she was on the river bank.
>
> "Thank you! Thank you!" she cried. "You saved my life."
>
> Later, the dove was sitting on the branch of a tree. A hunter came by and was going to shoot her. The dove didn't see the hunter but the little ant did. As the hunter fired, the ant bit his heel. The hunter jumped. He missed the dove. The dove was safe.
>
> "Thank you, dear ant, for saving my life," said the dove. "I'll never forget your kindness!". .

Here is part of a decodable text used for older students who are beyond beginning first grade level, but still do not know how to decode. Students have learned all of the sounds in all of the words in the text.

> The little boy was happy to see his sister. "I have a gift for you. The stranger gave it to me."
>
> "He's not a stranger, Tom. He's my friend. Would you like to come with me to the lodge by the lake?" she asked.
>
> "I would like to go," he answered. Tom and his sister trudged up the hill to the lodge and . . .

For students in Grades 4 and up, decodable texts are usually only necessary for the first few lessons.

Choose the right reading level

There are three broad reading levels that produce distinctly different results: the independent reading level, the instructional reading level, and the frustration reading level.

Independent Reading Level	Instructional Reading Level	Frustration Reading Level
easy	just right	too hard
Does not know 0 - 1 word	Does not know 2 - 5 words	Does not know 6 or more words

If a student has to figure out only one word, the book is too easy. If a student does not know six or more words, the book is too difficult. A student will *not* make adequate progress if the book is too easy or too difficult

1. **Independent reading level**

   Students will say the text is easy. They can read these fluently without any help. They understand what they have read. If you ask questions about the text, they can tell you the important facts with 90% accuracy. They only have to stop and figure out no more than one word per 100 words.

   Reading at this level has great benefits. It:

   - Increases fluency and accuracy in reading words.
   - Increases reading speed.
   - Fosters a love for reading because the task is easy.

   CAUTION: Reading at this level does NOT create maximum reading growth. If students only read at this level, their reading skills will *not* develop to the greatest potential.

2. **Frustration Reading Level**

   Texts at the frustration level are too difficult for students to read and comprehend. Six or more words per 100 are unknown or too difficult. Students may refuse to read, have difficulty pronouncing many words, use a finger to point at each word, or engage in word-by-word reading. By the time they finish the sentence or a paragraph, they do not know what they have read because so much effort has been spent on trying to read the words. If you ask questions about the text, students can only give a few details with less than 50% accuracy. A student might say, "I don't understand what I read. I don't like to read. I can't read it. It's too hard."

If students attempt to read at the frustration level:
- A hatred for reading develops that usually translates into a hatred for school.
- Vocabulary knowledge stalls.
- Fluency is interrupted.
- Comprehension plummets.
- The knowledge base does not grow.

*Students should NEVER read at the frustration level.
It is harmful for the student.*

3. **Instructional reading level**

   Texts at this level are easy for students when they have some help. Students only have to stop and figure out two to five words per hundred and they can answer questions about the text with about 70% accuracy. ***Maximum reading growth occurs at the instructional level.*** Texts can be those that students have to read for any subject or those they have chosen on their own.

Teach students how to know their reading level.

Show students how to choose a "just right" book by counting how many words they have to stop and figure out. Have them turn to the middle of the text where there are no pictures and begin reading. Have them raise a finger for every word they have to stop and figure out. One or no fingers raised means the text is too easy, two to five fingers means the book is "just right," and more than five means the text is too difficult. Have students read their selected text to you for a one or two minutes to make sure they are reading at the correct level.

The Five Finger Test

1 finger = too easy

2 - 5 fingers = just right

6+ fingers = too difficult

The exceptions

- When students are reading at a beginning first grade level, they may have to stop and figure out almost every word. That is okay. It is still at the instructional level since they know all the graphemes and can decode.

- Sometimes students insist on reading a text that is too difficult because it is of high interest to them. Under most circumstances, it is acceptable to allow them to read the text because their determination to read it will overshadow any frustration. They are determined to figure out the words and understand the content.

Provide time to read

Reading during school may seem like an obvious goal, but it is more difficult to achieve than one would suspect. Teachers battle for time for students to read. In a national survey, students read an *average* of *seven minutes* per day, not enough time to become skilled readers. Some students go to school every day and never read. How is it possible for a student to go to school and read little or not at all? Read these scenarios and decide how the student avoided reading.

Scenario #1

The teacher reads the story aloud while students follow along in their books. Good readers read and follow along, but many students do not. They just listen.

Scenario #2

The teacher has students take turns reading a sentence or paragraph while other students follow along. One student is reading, but most of the other students are trying to predict where they will be reading or are thinking about something else.

Scenario #3

The teacher reads the story and then has students respond to the story by drawing a picture, creating a bookmark, or other craft. Some refer to it as Language Arts and Crafts. In the average reading curriculum, there is 270 minutes of activities for every 20-minute story. Many times the emphasis is on the extras rather than reading itself.

Scenario #4

The teacher reads the story line by line, having students orally repeat each line together. Unfortunately, students can repeat the words without even looking at the text.

Scenario #5

When students are to be reading a story silently, poor students do not. They find other things to do, like disrupt their neighbor.

Scenario #6

When working in groups that require reading instructions, some students never read any of the instructions. They let their friends read them and then tell them what to do.

Between the opportunity to get away with not reading and the emphasis in the classroom on reading activities, it is possible for a student to go through an entire school day and never read a single word. The impact on the student who reads little is exponential.

The national average for time spent reading is seven minutes during the entire school day.

- **Students must read 30 minutes a day at the instructional level**

    In order to become proficient readers, students must read a minimum of 30 minutes a day at the instructional level. There are no shortcuts. If they don't read, they won't be proficient. If you are a classroom teacher, conduct a check for a week on how many minutes each students spends in actual reading. Reading activities don't count. If you are a parent, encourage your child to read daily.

- **Monitor the reading level and reading time.**

    If you are teaching the right content in the right sequence with the right instruction, almost all students will make rapid progress. That means that a text that was "just right" for the student last week, might be too easy this week. Students must be reading at the instructional level.

    When I work with students one-on-one or in a small group, I have students keep a reading log and bring it and their chosen book to each lesson. I can glance at the log and see how many pages they have read in the alloted time. I can also see how many and what kinds of words were difficult.

Title & Author	Date	Time	Page Numbers	Words I had to stop and figure out

As students become better readers, the number of pages increases and the number of difficult words decreases. Sometimes it dwindles to zero or only one. Then it is time to adjust the reading level so at least three to five words appear on the list. They will plateau in their reading if they stay at the "too easy" reading level. It is time for them to find a new text at the instructional level. I have students read their text to me for one to two minutes to make sure it is at the instructional level.

Tanya

Tanya, a student going into seventh grade, read at a beginning fourth grade level according to the *Woodcock Reading Mastery Test*. She was reading three grade levels below her grade. The first week, she chose a book at the beginning fourth grade level, but she had to change the level of her book almost every week. Within ten lessons, she was reading at a beginning seventh grade level.

The classroom dilemma

The problem: students need to learn the grade level material, but the required reading is at the frustration level. They can't read it well enough to gain meaning. This just deepens their hatred for reading and for school. Providing comprehension strategies does not alleviate the issue because they can't read the words in the first place. It is a difficult situation for both teachers and students. What are some possible solutions?

- Provide or find someone to teach students how to read with the right content in the right sequence with the right instruction as soon as possible. Find a tutor for the student. Even in ten lessons, students start doing much better in class.

- Also, provide alternate means for learning the content such as from video, audio, and internet resources. If students have access to these *before* class discussions and class work, they feel more confident in learning.

- Also, provide a way for students to read 30 minutes a day *at their instructional level.* This is absolutely critical for growth in reading skills, vocabulary, knowledge base, and interest in learning. Without reading, students will continue to fall further and further behind.

SPECIAL NOTE: It is tempting for teachers to read the text to the students and then assign students to read it. This practice is detrimental for three reasons:

1. ***It prevents students from using the tools of decoding.*** They do not get practice tackling unknown words and become dependent on others to tell them the words.

2. ***It encourages memorization of whole words.*** Many poor readers have brilliant memories and will just remember the words and store them on the right side of the brain. We want words to be processed phonologically and stored in the Word Center of the left brain.

3. ***Many students will not read the text themselves.*** The teacher has already done the work. This prevents students from engaging in enough reading time to become skilled readers. **Students need to read the text themselves first.**

Students who read more . . .
become more fluent,
learn more vocabulary,
have a better knowledge base,
and are more proficient at comprehension.

Chapter 14: The Secret to Thinking about Meaning

I keep six honest serving-men
(They taught me all I knew);
Their names are *What* and *Why* and *When*
And *How* and *Where* and *Who*.

-- Rudyard Kipling

What is reading comprehension?

Reading comprehension is the ability to gain information and meaning from the articles, stories, and books we read. That is the whole purpose of reading. It requires the ability to:

- Accurately and fluently read words.
- Connect what we read to prior experience and knowledge.
- Use powerful questions to unlock meaning

Accurately and fluently reading words.

When words have been processed through the language centers of the left brain, they are stored in the Word Center. They can be retrieved instantly which frees up working memory to concentrate on meaning. Phonemic awareness, grapheme knowledge, decoding, and fluency are the foundational skills for reading comprehension.

If students do not have this foundation, they may appear to have a reading comprehension problem, but that is not the root issue. These students have memorized a large number of words instead of processing them through the language centers of the left brain. So much working memory is used to read the words there is little left to focus on meaning. If we try to solve the problem by introducing comprehension strategies, there is usually little success. Students still struggle because the root cause has not been addressed.

What is the solution? ***Teach students the basic skills.*** They need phonemic awareness, knowledge of the graphemes, the ability to construct and decode words, and the ability to read fluently. Then along with this instruction, teach them comprehension skills using the instructional level texts they are reading.

Connecting with prior knowledge

Comprehension also requires the ability to connect prior knowledge to what we are reading. We use what we know to understand what we don't know. Background knowledge is one of the critical components of reading comprehension. In fact, the amount of prior knowledge a reader has about a topic indicates how much will be understood and remembered. Some poor readers have reasonable comprehension in spite of their weak foundational skills because they have a broad knowledge base. At the same time, some good readers may have poor reading comprehension because they lack background knowledge. These students can read all the words accurately and fluently but have no idea what they mean.

Here is an example. How much can you understand?

> Although the circular orbit theory of the Bohr model was successful in explaining the line spectrum of hydrogen-like atoms and the small wavelength shift arising from the relative motion of the nucleus, very precise measurements on hydrogen reveal that the energy levels have fine structure.
>
> Marshall L. Burns, Tuskegee University
> *Modern Physics For Science And Engineering*

You most likely can read every word accurately and fluently. If you have background knowledge in physics, you may understand it. If not, you can read it but have no idea what it means.

What does background knowledge do for you?

How does background knowledge impact comprehension? Here is another example. What words and phrases come to your mind when you read the name *Abraham Lincoln*. What floods your mind with just the name? If you are like most, you think tall, beard, top hat, Civil War, slavery issues, and President. You might even think of personal experiences in visiting historical places connected to him. These ideas and images are not just about the man himself, but also about what he did, the issues of the time period, your own personal experiences and attitudes, and general knowledge. For example, when you thought President, you also knew about the office of President of the United States and the duties that it entails. Your background knowledge is a web of interrelated descriptions, concepts, emotions, and attitudes that comes from years of reading, conversations, and experiences related to Abraham Lincoln.

The more detailed and complex your understanding of a topic, the easier it is to process new information and incorporate it into your existing knowledge base. If you were to read a speech or a story about Abraham

Lincoln, all that background knowledge would influence how you created meaning from the text.

Visualization

Although visualization is a strategy often intended to help students comprehend text, it may not be as effective as we thought. If we have background knowledge of a topic, we automatically visualize the information. If we do not have a knowledge base of the topic, visualization is difficult.

> "Proficient readers **spontaneously and purposefully** create mental images while and after they read. The images emerge from all five senses, as well as the emotions, and are anchored in a reader's **prior knowledge**... Proficient readers use images to draw conclusions, to create distinct and unique interpretations of the text, to recall details significant to the text, and to recall a text after it has been read."
>
> Keene & Zimmerman
> *Mosaic of Thought: Teaching Comprehension*

The mental images are the *product* of comprehension flowing out of background knowledge. If you know little or nothing about a topic, it is difficult to visualize anything.

How do we build a broad knowledge base?

The process of building background knowledge begins early in life. Parents who read to their children and engage in discussions about texts and the environment are building a foundation for reading comprehension. In contrast, children who come to school without that experience usually lack a strong knowledge base for understanding text. This makes it critical that once students enter school, focus must be on building that broad knowledge base.

What about vocabulary?

Vocabulary and background knowledge are inseparable twins. We usually don't have one without the other. To describe knowledge, we use vocabulary.

The more specific and detailed the content area, the more technical the words used to communicate that knowledge.

Most vocabulary is learned through engaging in purposeful conversations and reading. That means when children have limited interactions with parents and teachers or when reading is limited, vocabulary growth suffers or even stalls.

The power of listening vocabulary

Our listening vocabulary consists of words we never speak, read, or write, but we know them from listening to others. Conversations about texts and the world build our listening vocabulary.

It is our listening vocabulary that impacts our ability to understand text, decode multisyllable words, and decode words that break the rules. The more words we read and hear, the larger our listening vocabulary becomes. That is why worksheets and utility conversations such as, "*Put the toys away,*" do not substantially contribute to it.

- *Listening vocabulary helps us understand the meaning of a text.* If students are skilled at reading words and have a good listening vocabulary, they will be able to understand a text even when it contains words they never use while speaking or writing. They often know what those words mean and can interpret the meaning of the text.

- *Listening vocabulary helps us decode big words.* Knowing how to pronounce multisyllable words can present a problem. As we saw in Chapter 10, pronunciation gets tricky because vowels can change from long to short or short to long when we add suffixes. The stressed syllable can also change, completely changing the pronunciation.

    However, if the word is in my listening vocabulary, I can tell from the context what the word is, although I have never written, spoken, or read it before. If it is not in my listening vocabulary, my only other option is to have someone tell me the word or skip it. Most students are unlikely to look up a word in a dictionary to find the meaning or the pronunciation.

- *Listening vocabulary helps us decode words that break the rules.* If students attempt to decode a word that does not follow the rules, they can often quickly adjust it to the correct word based on their listening vocabulary. For example, the word *yacht* would be impossible to "sound out." However, if the word is in my listening vocabulary I can say "y-ă –k-t," realize it is close to a word I already know that fits the context of rich people sailing on the ocean, and pronounce it correctly. I hear students say, "I didn't know that was what the word looked like!" They knew the word; they had just never seen it in print before.

Young children use this process to adjust the pronunciation of common words like *said* and *there*. The word *there* may momentarily be pronounced *theer*, but quickly adjusted to the correct pronunciation. Students with a good listening vocabulary are more likely to vary the pronunciation of an unknown word to read it correctly.

Vocabulary and comprehension

Vocabulary development affects the ability to comprehend a text. Some children enter first grade knowing 8000 root words while some only know 4000 root words. Research has shown that these vocabulary differences in first grade impact high school reading comprehension scores. The consequences are long-term.

It is not possible to teach the 3500 words that students need to learn each year. Instead, students must engage in massive amounts of reading and in deep conversations about texts and the world around them. That is how we learn most vocabulary.

Strategies for building a knowledge base and vocabulary

Here are some strategies that can help students make substantial gains in background knowledge and vocabulary.

- **Read aloud to students.**

    This applies to all lower and upper elementary grades. Include books that students would not be able to read on their own. Choose books that will build a knowledge base in a broad spectrum of content and life experiences. Engage students in meaningful conversations about the text using the vocabulary of the content.

- **Give students opportunity to read at their instructional level.**

    Volume counts. Give students access to a wide variety of books through the classroom libraries, school libraries, and public libraries. Then give them the opportunity to read these books for at least 30 minutes a day. The more they read, the more knowledge and vocabulary they will gain. This reading must be at the instructional level.

- **Teach units on specific topics.**

    Teach units of knowledge with carefully selected books and activities that provide detailed, systematic content on a topic. By teaching a unit, vocabulary is repeated which helps place those words into long term memory. Engage students in meaningful conversations about the text using that vocabulary. Worksheets *do not* develop comprehension and vocabulary as well as conversations.

- **Choose groups of books on a single topic.**

    If you are having students mainly read isolated texts with unrelated content, one immediate remedy is to group books by content area and teach a systematic, detailed unit on a topic. In each subject area, integrate picture books, stories, biographies, historical fiction, and informational texts to enable students to build a broad knowledge base on particular subject. You can also choose texts on topics students already know. Take the foundation of their current knowledge base and build new understanding on it.

- **Go on field trips, real or virtual.**

    Field trips provide detailed, interesting information on specific topics. Before the experience, prepare students by asking questions and having them read on the topic. After the field trip, engage them in reflective conversations about the experience.

Connecting to what we know

It is not enough to have background knowledge. We must know that the knowledge we have applies to the text at hand. Although students may have some background in a topic or a related subject, they may not realize what they are reading is related to what they already know. We have to help them make that connection to what they already know.

- *Before reading.* Design an activity that leads students to think about the knowledge base for understanding the text. It may be a single question asked before reading, or it may be an extended activity that takes an entire class period. Activities that require an individual response from each student are more effective than those that require a response from single individual within a group.

- *During and after reading.* Use powerful questions to help students make the connection between what they know and what they don't know.

Using powerful questions to unlock meaning

How do we gain information from a text? The secret is powerful questions. Use *who, what, when, where, why,* and *how* questions to help students discover the information within the text. As students hear you ask well-worded questions, **they will begin asking themselves those same kind of questions** as they read. They will learn to think while they are reading.

Be careful! The task of writing questions depends upon you. Don't rely upon questions that accompany texts because they may be designed to *test* rather than to *develop thinking processes*. You may have to write your own.

Guidelines for powerful questions

- *Begin questions with who, what, when, where, why, and how.*

- *Mainly ask questions that begin with what, why, and how.* These types of questions help students think about meaning and not just about the simple facts of *who, what, when* or *where*.

- *Avoid yes/no questions.* There are rare occasions when these types of questions are valuable, but most of the time they do not generate deep thought. When you stop and think about it, the real answer to questions beginning with *do, is, can, etc.* is actually "Yes" or "No." Also, avoid asking a yes/no question and then tacking on *"Why or why not."* You will have a broader, better question if you reword it to start with *why, what*, or *how*.

- *Avoid questions that add unnecessary words* such as, "Who can tell me....?" or "Does any know...?" These extra words dramatically slow the pace of a discussion and add nothing to comprehension.

- *Design questions that require students to look at patterns in the text.* We want students to be able to pull information out of the text and think about the significance of the patterns they see. We want students to think about:

    - Repetition of words, phrases, and ideas
    - Sequence of events or actions
    - Cause and effect
    - Comparison and contrast

- *Ask questions that help students make thoughtful inferences* from the information in the text.

    "Why do you think...?"
    "What does this tell you about...?

FACTS	PATTERNS	INFERENCES
Who? What? When? Where? Why? How?	Repetition Sequence Cause and effect Comparison and contrast	Conclusions based on the facts and patterns

- *To help you prepare powerful questions, it is helpful to write statements about the facts and inferences first.* Then turn those statements into well-worded questions. In essence, you are writing the answer before you write the question. Some questions should require students to combine facts in order to answer the question.

- *Always write out the answer.* The question may sound great but may not actually have a good answer. You may be surprised that some of your questions may have simple answers, are too confusing to answer, or have no answer at all.

- *Revise your questions if necessary.* Rewrite them until they encourage thoughtful answers. Asking good questions does not come naturally. It takes practice.

Two types of questions

To develop critical thinking skills, we need to ask two types of questions. Those with answers found directly in the text provide a foundation for critical thinking. Without the facts, the conclusions are meaningless. Those with answers beyond the text encourage students to think about the meaning and implications.

Answers in the text	Answers beyond the text
Answers to the question are found on the page	Answers to the questions are *not* found on the page
Provides foundation for meaning	Encourages thinking about meaning

Here is the story of *The Two Frogs* with two possible sets of questions. What are the differences between the two sets of questions?

The Two Frogs

Two frogs lived by a lake. One spring it was so hot that the lake dried up. There was no more water. The frogs needed to find water some other place. They hopped and hopped to find something to drink. Soon they came to a deep well with some water at the bottom.

"I want to jump in," said one frog. "I want a drink."

"No! No!" cried the other frog. "I want a drink, too, but this well is too deep. We can jump into the well but can we jump out of the well?"

Question Set #1	Analysis
• How many frogs were there?	2 - One word answer
• <u>Can you tell me</u> why the lake dried up?	Yes/no, extra words
• What was at the bottom of the well?	water - One word answer
• <u>Does anyone know</u> why the first frog wanted to jump into the well?	Yes/no, extra words
• <u>Do</u> you think the second frog was right? Why or why not?	Yes/no, better to reword

146   Chapter 14 / Thinking about Meaning

This set of questions does not promote thinking about the story. Most of the questions are yes/no questions or only require a one word answer..

Here is a second set of questions that uses the guidelines for powerful questions.

Question Set #2	Answers
• Why did the frogs have to leave the lake? • *If needed, help students extend their answer.* How would a dry lake affect the frogs?	• *It was hot one spring and the lake dried up.* • *They would have nothing to drink and frogs like to swim.*
• How could the hot weather cause the lake to dry up?	• *The heat causes the water to evaporate.*
• Why did one frog want to jump into the well? (What is a well?)	• *He wanted a drink. He must have been very thirsty.*
• <u>What</u> did the second frog think would happen if they jumped into the well?	• *He didn't think they would be able to get out of the well.*
• <u>What</u> does this tell you about a well?	• *The water in the well must be a long way down.*
• <u>Why</u> do you think it would be easier to jump into a well than to get out of a well?	• *The frogs could fall into the well, but couldn't jump high enough to get out.*
• Both frogs made a decision. <u>Which</u> decision was better? <u>What</u> made it better?	• *The second frog was thinking ahead to the consequences and not just thinking about getting a drink.*

Look at the difference between the two sets of questions. Notice that most of the questions begin with what, what, and how. The second set requires more thought about the setting and the characters. ***This set develops critical thinking skills.*** The first set of questions does not.

In Summary

1. Reading comprehension requires the ability to:
   - Accurately and fluently read words.
   - Connect what we read to prior experience and knowledge.
   - Use powerful questions to unlock meaning

2. Powerful questions unlock the meaning of a text.
   - Begin questions with *who, what, when, where, why,* and *how*.
   - Mainly ask questions that begin with *what, why*, and *how*
   - Avoid yes/no questions.
   - Avoid questions that add unnecessary words .
   - Design questions that look for repetition, sequence, cause and effect, comparison and contrast
   - Ask questions with answers *in* the text and questions that require thinking **beyond** the text.

Chapter 15: The Secret to Writing about Meaning

**Writing is a tool for
thinking about meaning.**

Writing about meaning

Students need to be able to lift information out of text by asking *who, what, when, where, why* and *how*. Writing about the text they are reading is an effective way to do this. A well-designed writing assignment that requires students to look for the facts, identify patterns, and make inferences strengthens critical thinking skills.

Writing is thinking on paper.

Always have students begin writing with a piece that is *short enough* to be revised and edited easily. For students who do not like to read and write, this is important. The goal is to ensure success at every level. We usually have students write too much.

Before I learned this principle, my students would write and write and write. There were so many errors and so many parts that had to be revised that it was impossible to make the corrections. If I asked students to look at their work, they became discouraged at the insurmountable task. Neither the students nor I enjoyed it.

So how long should the piece be? Just long enough for students to revise and edit it in a reasonable amount of time. The better writers they become, the longer the piece can be. Start with one sentence or a question with a one sentence answer. When students can write the perfect sentence, teach them how to write one paragraph. When students can write one paragraph with few or no errors, teach them how to write three paragraphs, then five paragraphs, and finally longer reports. As students learn the skills, they make fewer and fewer errors so in the end a five paragraph essay has no more errors than the one sentence or one paragraph did at the beginning.

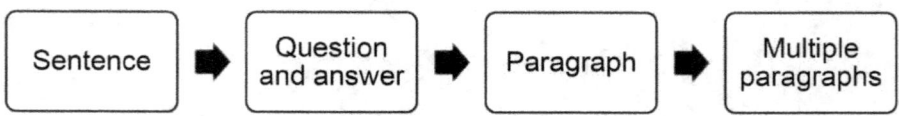

Guidelines for all writing assignments

- *Choose an appropriate assignment.* Start with an assignment that only requires students to write a sentence or a question and a one sentence answer. When students understand the sentence, teach them how to write the paragraph.

- *Guide students in planning their writing.* Model the process until you know students understand and can complete the assignment on their own. Do an example with them.

- *Assign students to write the piece on their own.*

- *Have students proofread their piece and fix it.* Show students how to use the Self-check List to edit their work. Students will use this after they complete their piece to "fix" any errors before you see it.

Self-check List

1. Whisper read your writing.
2. Did you leave out any words?
3. Do you have a capital letter at the beginning of every sentence?
4. Is there a capital letter at the beginning of every name?
5. Is that the only place there are capitals?
6. Is there end punctuation at the end of each sentence?
7. Underline the words that you are not sure how to spell.
8. Find out how to spell them and correct them.
9. Correct any other errors you see.

- *Check student work and give them feedback.* After students have finished writing and editing their work, then it is time for you to look at their writing. If there are errors, guide students in fixing those. Use the principles of errorless learning and immediate feedback, asking students questions and giving them clues. ***The pencil always stays in the hand of the student.*** Do not make corrections on student papers. Just point them out or lightly mark where those errors are.

The goal: a piece with perfect grammar, spelling, and punctuation that shows reflective thought.

This process can occur over two or three days. I usually assign the writing and model some suggestions. Students then plan, write, proofread, and "fix" errors on their own. When that is completed, we look at the papers together and students make further revisions until the piece is correct.

The Perfect Sentence

All beginning readers and all poor readers, no matter what their age, must spend some time getting acquainted with the sentence. Many will not know the difference between a complete and incomplete sentence. Many will not know when to use a capital letter. Some will intersperse capital letters throughout a sentence, even in the middle of a word.

Capital letters come at the beginning of a sentence
and at the beginning of the name
of anyone, any place, or anything.

The oral sentence

Students in kindergarten, first grade and those just learning English will need to begin with the oral sentence. After students have engaged in word building, help them construct an oral sentence using one of the words.

- Choose a word that students have just built.
- Ask them to think of a sentence using that word.
- Call on one student to say a sentence.
- Help the student extend the sentence by asking questions

STUDENT: He found a stick. *(The word is stick.)*

TEACHER: <u>Who</u> found the stick?

STUDENT: Jamie found the stick.

TEACHER: <u>Where</u> did Jamie find the stick?

STUDENT: Jamie found the stick on the ground.

TEACHER: <u>Where</u> on the ground?

STUDENT: Jamie found the stick on the ground in his backyard.

TEACHER: <u>When</u> did Jamie find the stick?

STUDENT: Yesterday, Jamie found the stick on the ground in his backyard.

Notice you are helping students think of *who, what, when* and *where*. In other sentences you may also use *why* and *how*. This lays the foundation for pulling information out of a text. It develops a way of thinking.

The written sentence

These students also need to be writing a sentence at the same time they are practicing the oral sentence. This sentence will be a response to the text they are reading. It may be an answer to a question you ask or about a person, object, or event they choose from the text. The following are the steps that students will use in constructing the sentence.

Step 1: Generate ideas.

    What do you know about the person, object, or event?
    What do you know about the question you were asked?
    Make a list.

Step 2: Use the Sentence Frame.

    Use the Sentence Frame to help you write a strong sentence. Write one, two or three words or a phrase in each box. You may not need all of the boxes.

The Sentence Frame

Who/What?	Did What?	When?
Where?	Why?	How?

Step 3: Write the sentence.

    Use the words in the boxes to write a strong sentence. You may have to put the words in a different order. You may decide not to use all the words.

Step 4: Check your work and fix it.

    Use the Self-check List to help you find your mistakes. Fix them. *After students finish editing their sentence, check their work. Guide students in fixing any additional errors.*

An example

Goldilocks and the Three Bears

Why did Goldilocks always choose baby bear's things?

*(This may be a question the teacher asks or
a question the student asks when reading the story)*

Who/What?	Did What?	When?
Goldilocks	chose baby bear's porridge, chair, bed	
Where?	**Why?**	**How?**
house	just right	

Goldilocks chose baby bears' porridge, chair, and bed when she was in the bear's house because his things were just right.

When Goldilocks was in the bear's house, she chose baby bears' porridge, chair, and bed because his things were just right.

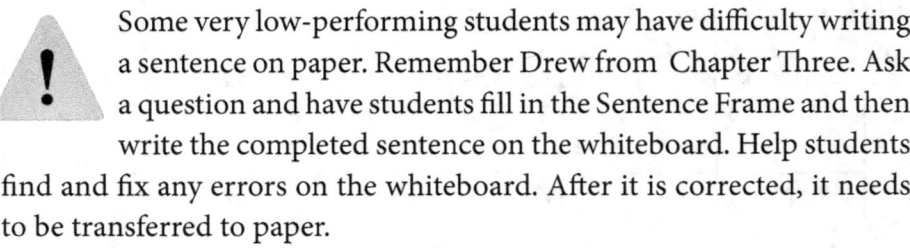 Some very low-performing students may have difficulty writing a sentence on paper. Remember Drew from Chapter Three. Ask a question and have students fill in the Sentence Frame and then write the completed sentence on the whiteboard. Help students find and fix any errors on the whiteboard. After it is corrected, it needs to be transferred to paper.

The question and one sentence answer

Students in 4th grade and up can usually write both the question and a one sentence answer from the very beginning. Younger readers usually skip this step and can be shown how to write a paragraph after they have mastered the sentence.

In the question and answer assignments, students pretend to be the teacher and write a good question that begins with *how, what,* or *why.* They then answer it in one sentence. Students usually do not have much difficulty writing a question. However the one-sentence answer is usually a problem.

Use the guidelines for all writing assignments. Model the process orally with students until you know they understand and can complete the assignment. They need to see how you. . .

- think about the text,
- ask a question,
- write out the question,
- use the Sentence Frame to plan the answer, and then
- write out the answer in a complete sentence.

Students will complete this assignment as homework and bring it to the next lesson. When students bring the question and answer, help them revise and edit if necessary. Let them make the corrections themselves on their own paper. *The pen always stays in the hand of the student.*

The "What" question. . .

Pretend you are the teacher.
Write one good "what" question about your book. "What. . .?"
Then answer your question in a complete sentence.

The "How" question. . .

Pretend you are the teacher.
Write one good "how" question about your book. "How. . . .?"
Then answer your question in a complete sentence.

The "Why" question. . .

Pretend you are the teacher.
Write one good "why" question about your book. "Why. . . .?"
Then answer your question in a complete sentence.

The paragraph

Once students have mastered the sentence, they are ready to learn how to write different types of paragraphs. Understanding the elements of the single paragraph is necessary not only for writing, but also for reading comprehension. Learning the organization of paragraphs is best done by constructing them rather than reading them.

These students are usually just learning how to write a well-constructed paragraph. A simple step-by-step procedure and a paragraph frame can be used to guide them. The following basic structure is used for most types of paragraphs with slight differences in the type of information that goes into each section.

- Topic sentence
- Supporting detail 1
- Supporting detail 2
- Supporting detail 3
- Concluding sentence

Guide students through the following steps in constructing a paragraph. Demonstrate each step by writing a sample paragraph with them. Then guide students in using these steps on their own.

Step 1: Gather information.

Who? What? When? Where? Why? How?

The type of information gathered will depend upon the type of paragraph students are writing.

Provide a graphic organizer for students to record their information.

Step 2: Organize it.

The graphic organizers will help you find and organize the information.

Step 3: Write the topic sentence.

This is a summary of the important ideas. Use the Sentence Frame to write the topic sentence.

Step 4: Find three reasons why the topic sentence is true.

These details are in the information that was organized.

Step 5: Put the three reasons in order.

These reasons can just be numbered on the graphic organizer.

Step 6: Write at least one sentence for each reason.

Use the Sentence Frame if necessary. Every sentence must tell who or what and what happened.

Step 7: Write the concluding sentence.

The concluding sentence shows that the writer is finished. It pulls together the main idea into a single sentence. Take the topic sentence and write it in a different order. Use different words that mean the same thing. Don't introduce any new ideas.

Step 8 :Write your paragraph neatly.

Now write your paragraph.
- Indent the first line. Write every other line so you have space above the words to fix any errors later.
- Use words like *first, second, since, because, due to, also, therefore, as a result,* or *consequently.*

Step 9: Check your work and fix it.

After you finish writing your paragraph, check it and make the corrections. Use the Self-check list to help you find your mistakes.

Step 10: Make final corrections.

Make any final corrections your teacher finds.

Students should be able to follow these steps on their own once you have modeled the type of paragraph to be written. When they bring their paragraph to the next lesson, help them revise and edit if necessary. Let them make the corrections themselves on their own paper. The pen always stays in the hand of the student. Guide them in producing a well-written paragraph.

Here are some of the types of paragraphs you may want to introduce to students. Most of these can be used with any text they have chosen to read for 30 minutes a day.

- Cause and effect paragraph
- How to
- Comparison
- Contrast
- Comparison and contrast (usually two paragraphs)
- Description of character, setting, or object
- Informational
- Opinion
- Persuasion
- Sequence of time, events

Paragraph frames

A paragraph frame is a helpful tool for students just learning how to write a paragraph. After identifying the information, students can write the information in the frame.

Sample frame for compare and contrast paragraphs

```
_____ and _____ are alike in many ways. First, _____
_____. Next, _____. They
also _____. Finally_____.
_____ and _____ are also different in many ways. First,
_____. Next,
_____. They also _____.
Finally, _____.
_____ and _____ have more (similarities/ differences)
than (similarities/ differences).
```

Students then recopy the paragraph on their own paper so it appears just as if they had written it completely on their own. This way they must pay attention to capitalization, punctuation, and formatting. They need to indent the paragraph and skip every other line for easy editing.

Why is writing so important?

Writing is not just an end in itself. The value in writing extends to all of the language arts.

- *It is a way to learn text structure.*

    One of the foundational prerequisites for reading comprehension is understanding text structure. The most effective way to teach this is by having students write their own pieces. For example, they learn comparison and contrast by writing comparison and contrast.

- *It is a way to refine knowledge of grammar and sentence structure.*

    Writing provides a tangible way to manipulate words into correct order with correct usage. Students can become brilliant writers. Those who are learning the English language or who come from literacy deprived environments benefit from explicitly paying attention to structure.

- *It is a way to develop thinking.*

    Students learn how to express themselves logically, supporting their ideas with details. They may be expressing their own ideas or responding to the ideas of others. Either way, they develop skills to communicate what they understand effectively.

- *It is a way to learn how to spell.*

    Students learn to read by spelling, but they learn to spell by writing. This is where real spelling instruction takes place. Many students do not learn to spell by memorizing spelling lists for spelling tests, but they do learn to spell through their own writing if they make their own corrections.

- *It is a way to expand vocabulary.*

    Writing provides an opportunity to use words from their listening vocabulary and not just speaking vocabulary. By using the words they hear but don't speak, their vocabulary expands.

- *It is a way to learn reading comprehension skills.*

    Skills used in learning to write can be used in reverse to comprehend text. Attempts to teach students these same skills through reading comprehension strategies alone often fail because students are not engaged in the construction process. It is much more challenging to look at someone else's writing and try to reconstruct what the author did. However, if students have gone through the writing process themselves, it is much easier to spot those same processes when reading. Once you have done it yourself, you understand it much better.

The Cause and Effect Paragraph

NAME_____

Stories make more sense when we understand why things happen and what makes them happen. A cause is an event, feeling or action that makes something happen. The thing that happens is the effect.

Step 1: Gather information

Who? What? When? Where? Why? How?

Find an event. List all the possible reasons why this event happened.

What happened (the effect)	Why it happened (the cause)

Step 2: Organize it.

Look at your list. What information is important?
Put the information in order. What causes were most important?
Choose one thing that happened.

Step 3: Write the topic sentence.

This is a summary of what happened. This will tell me what you are going to explain. Use the Sentence Frame to write the topic sentence.

Who?	*What?*	*When?*
Where?	*Why?*	*How?*

Step 4: Find three or more causes for the event.

These details are in the information that was organized.

Step 5: Put these causes in order. Just number them.

Step 6: Write at least one sentence for each cause.

Use the Sentence Frame if necessary. Every sentence must tell who or what and what happened.

Step 7: Write the conclusion sentence by rewording the topic sentence.

Write the sentence in a different order. Use different words that mean the same thing. Don't introduce any new ideas.

The Cause and Effect Paragraph

Step 8: Write your paragraph.

Now it is time to write your whole paragraph. Use the paragraph frame to give you ideas on how to organize your paragraph.

Paragraph Frame

In _____, _____
(name of book or story)   (tell what happened).
_____. This happened because _____. Also, _____. As a result, _____.

Step 9: Write your paragraph neatly.

- Now write your paragraph without the frame.
- Indent the first line.
- Write every other line so you can edit it easily later.
- Use words like *first, second, since, because, due to, also, therefore, as a result,* or *consequently*.

Step 10: Check your work and fix it.

After you finish writing your paragraph, check it and make the corrections. Use the Self-check list to help you find your errors.

Self-check List

1. Read your writing out loud.
2. Did you leave out any words?
3. Do you have a capital letter at the beginning of every sentence?
4. Is there a capital letter at the beginning of every name?
5. Is that the only place there are capitals?
6. Is there end punctuation at the end of each sentence?
7. Underline the words that you are not sure how to spell.
8. Find out how to spell them and correct them.
9. Correct any other errors you see.

In Summary

1. Have students write only as much as they can successfully revise and edit.

2. Gradually increase the amount of writing.
   - The perfect sentence
   - The question and one sentence answer
   - The Paragraph
   - Three paragraphs
   - Five paragraphs
   - Multiple paragraphs

3. Have students use these steps for writing.
   - Gather information.
   - Organize it.
   - Write.
   - Self-check their own work and fix it.
   - Check students work and let them fix it.

4. The pencil/pen stays in the hand of the student.

Chapter 16: Assessing Foundational Skills

**Know exactly which skills
each student has and does not have.**

If we are to help students progress in reading, we must know *exactly* how well students know the right content.

The Right Instruction	• Errorless learning and immediate feedback • Confidence that students can achieve • Kinesthetic strategies for every concept.
The Right Content	• Hear the individual sounds in spoken words • Know the spellings of the 42-44 speech sounds • Put sounds and spellings together to form words • Know how to add prefixes and suffixes • Be able to decode small and big words • Read smoothly with expression • Think about meaning
The Right Sequence	• The sequence the brain uses in processing words

Assessing the right content provides a systematic way to discover the source of a reading problem. No matter what the presenting problem might be, we have to make sure all of the foundational skills are in place. When those are addressed, many times the presenting issue disappears.

Assessing the right content provides a systematic way to discover the source of a reading problem.

Why do we need to assess?

Kids can fool you. They can know it and you think they don't. Or, they don't know it and you think they do. A kindergarten student might not respond when you show alphabet flash cards or might have a difficult time writing letters. However, when given letter tiles and instructed to find certain letters, surprisingly, the child can name them and give the sounds. All that was needed was a kinesthetic way to express what was known.

Some students appear to be reading well in the early grades, but in reality, they may have memorized all the words, have no phonemic awareness, and know only about half of the spellings of the phonemes. Unless students are assessed specifically for the foundational skills, no one will know until it is too late.

Any student, no matter what the age, that does not like to read, has a reading comprehension problem, has a fluency issue, or has been identified with some kind disability such as writing disabled or learning disabled needs to be assessed for the foundational skills. What appears to be the problem may not be the real issue. It is important to know what skills students have and do not have.

Assessment is not just a single moment in time when students are given a particular test, although it does include that. Assessment occurs every day as you evaluate what students know and do not know as they play the phonemic awareness games, spell the words, read aloud, and write. Continually monitor student progress in learning these skills.

The Framework for Teaching Reading

The Framework for Teaching Reading is my guide for teaching and assessing students. I need to know which skills are weak and which skills are strong. It provides a road-map of skills and the order in which they are acquired. Each skill on the Framework is necessary to become a successful reader. If a skill is weak, then each *successive* skill will be weak or nonexistent and the reading process breaks down. For example, if a student struggles with reading comprehension or fluency, but does not have phonemic awareness or know the graphemes, the student will make very little progress if I only address comprehension and fluency and not the missing skills of phonemic awareness and grapheme knowledge.

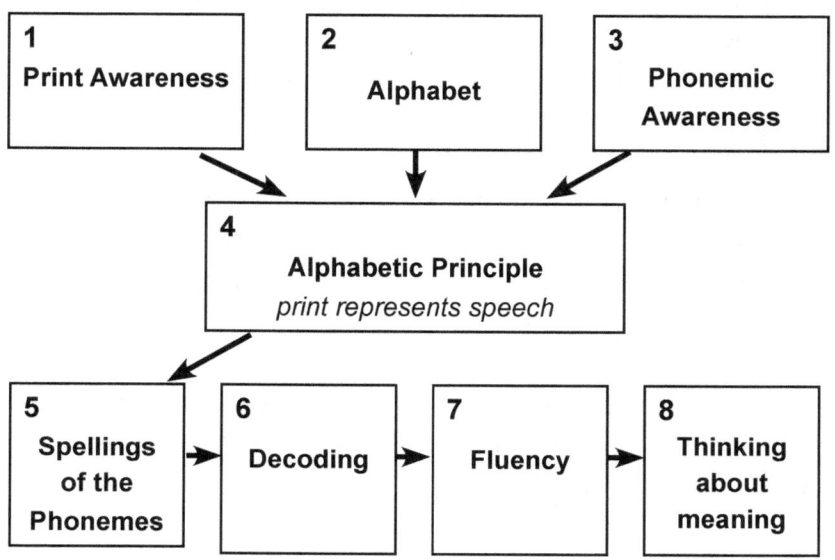

Framework for Teaching Reading

1. Print Awareness

This is understanding that written words and sentences convey meaning It is also knowing how to hold a book and understanding that we read from left to right and top to bottom,

2. Alphabet

I test Kindergarten, early Grade 1, and those just learning the language for alphabet knowledge. Almost all students in Grades 2 and up know the alphabet even if they can read only a handful of words.

3. Phonemic awareness

Older struggling readers usually know the alphabet, but they are usually lacking in phonemic awareness. I must know the level of phonemic awareness that students have and quickly bring them up to all six levels.

4. Alphabetic principle

The alphabetic principle is understanding the relationship between the sounds in speech and the letters on the page. Many students who can't hear the sounds in words don't know there is any relationship between the spoken word and the written word. To them, the letters on the page are arbitrary symbols.

5. Spellings of the Phonemes

I also must know what graphemes students know and do not know. Many older struggling readers do not know the spellings of the vowel sounds *oi, ou,* or *aw* or some of the more complex spellings of consonants and long vowels. I also must know whether students understand prefixes and suffixes, how to spell them and how to add them.

6. Decoding.

I must know whether students can decode an unknown word. Do they know how to break a word apart or do they just guess? They must be able to decode simple words as well as multisyllable words.

7. Fluency

I observe fluency but I do not address it until other critical areas are addressed. Fluency is easy to teach once students are storing words in the Word Center.

8. *Thinking about meaning*

As soon as students are able to read connected text, even if it is only one sentence, they need to be introduced to the higher-level skills of fluency and thinking about meaning. These need to be added to the instruction while students continue to work on the lower level skills.

Four basic assessments

Four basic assessments will help determine how well students have these foundational reading skills. Some of these can be incorporated into daily activities to provide ongoing information on the progress of students:

1. **Letter Recognition Test.** This test is for students in Kindergarten, early Grade 1, and those who are just learning the language. It assesses both name and sound recognition.

2. **Developmental Spelling Test.** This test assesses Phonemic Awareness Levels 1-4, knowledge of graphemes, prefixes, and suffixes, and understanding of the "Real Rules" of English that are found in Appendix C.

3. **Phonemic Awareness Tests.** These assess Phonemic Awareness Levels 1 - 5. They include the Phoneme Segmentation Assessment, The Phoneme Manipulation Assessment, and the Sound Card Assessment.

4. **Informal Reading Analysis.** This test assesses reading level, how students attack unknown words, and fluency.

What You Need To Know About A Student

Right Content	Question	Grade
Letter and sounds	1. What letters and sounds does the student know?	K–1
	2. What letters and sounds does the student not know?	K–1
Phonemic awareness	3. Does the student hear the beginning sound in words?	K–12
	4. Does the student hear the end sound in words?	K–12
	5. Does the student hear the middle vowel sound in words?	K–12
	6. Can the student hear each individual sound in a word?	K–12
	7. Can the student manipulate sounds in words?	K–12
Spellings of the sounds	8. What graphemes beyond the alphabet does the student know?	1–12
	9. What graphemes beyond the alphabet does the student not know?	1–12
Word building	10. Can the student listen to a spoken word and build the word?	K–12
	11. Does the student know how to add suffixes? prefixes? Which ones?	1–12
Decoding	12. Can the student decode a small word?	K–12
	13. Can the student decode a "big" word?	1–12
	14. Can the student read? At what level?	K–12
Fluency	15. Can the student read smoothly?	1–12
Thinking while reading	16. Can the student lift information out of a text?	K–12
	17. Can the student explain what they have read?	K–12

The Letter Recognition Test

Materials:

Set of lowercase alphabet cards arranged *in the order of the letters on the record sheet.*

Procedure:

> • "When I show you a letter, tell me the name of the letter and the sound."

If the student needs prompting:

> • "What is the name of the letter?
> • What is the sound?"

Letter Recognition Record Sheet

For an incorrect response, mark −

	Name	Sound
h		
l		
s		
e		
m		
r		
d		
f		
k		
n		
t		
x		
q		

	Name	Sound
c		
g		
i		
y		
u		
b		
j		
p		
a		
w		
o		
z		
v		

The Developmental Spelling Test

The Developmental Spelling Test is a powerful screening tool that identifies poor readers or those who are at risk for poor reading. It is administered as a regular spelling test, *but scored differently.* It provides a wealth of information on the foundational skills, including letter knowledge, phonemic awareness, understanding of the alphabetic principle, knowledge of graphemes, the ability to add prefixes and suffixes, and understanding of the "Real Rules" of English. These skills are missing in poor readers no matter what the age. To address the needs of these students, they must be distinguished from readers who only have weaknesses in fluency or comprehension. These two distinct groups require significantly different approaches to solving their reading problems.

The basis for this test is rooted in decades of research with thousands of children. It is founded on the stages of spelling development that reveals how much awareness a student has of the relationship between the speech sound and its representation in print. Because of this, the stages of spelling development become an important diagnostic tool for determining how much progress a student has made in learning the foundational skills and what further instruction needs to occur.

Administering the test

- Select the test that matches the grade level of the student and *not* the reading level. For example, if a student is in fourth grade and reading at a first-grade level, choose the test for fourth grade.

- *Students don't study the words ahead of time.*

- Give the test in the same manner as a regular spelling test to a whole classroom for screening purposes or to an individual student.

- Tell students to do the best they can and that words are not counted right or wrong. They get credit for every letter that is correct.

- Say the word, use it in a sentence, and then say the word again.

- The Developmental Spelling Test can be used to assess growth in Grade 1 and screen for remedial readers in Grades 2 - 12. Rarely will you have a poor reader with a visual memory good enough to score well on the test.

Developmental Spelling Lists

	Grade 1	Grades 2, 3	Grades 4, 5	Grades 6–12
1.	back	track	basket	packaging
2.	sink	switched	pitcher	literature
3.	mail	wrong	belonging	successful
4.	dress	when	dentist	destination
5.	picking	crunch	questions	cucumber
6.	lake	place	publicly	replacement
7.	rice	skating	placement	investigate
8.	peeked	screams	inflated	argument
9.	stamp	crawled	partner	awesome
10.	sold	brook	awful	mistook
11.	light	germ	bookkeepers	torment
12.	seed	thirsty	ordered	permanently
13.	dragon	choices	certainly	confirmation
14.	stick	houses	confirm	poisonous
15.	side	true	ointment	bountiful
16.	feet	phone	proudly	avenue
17.	bed	quiet	value	physician
18.	gate	circle	elephant	equipment
19.	test	gem	quail	participated
20.	pen	morning	circus	gigantic

**The Developmental Spelling Test
is a powerful screening tool.**

It a can be used for:
   whole classrooms, small groups, or individuals.

It identifies:
   weak phonemic awareness skills, lack of grapheme knowledge, and poor understanding of the "Real Rules" of English.

Scoring the Developmental Spelling Test

Students are scored on how accurately they represent the speech sounds.

- **You first look at only the beginning, end, and middle vowel sounds of a word.**

    Does the grapheme represent the speech sound? It is okay if the student uses the wrong grapheme if it still represents the sound. For example, they might use *ai* instead of *ay* or they might use *oi* instead of *oy*. If the grapheme represents the sound, you give credit. If a student uses *io* or *o* to represent the *oi*, it is incorrect because *io* or *o* never represent the sound /oi/.

- **Then look to see if <u>all</u> the sounds are represented by a grapheme that makes that sound.**

    Are there any missing sounds? Are there any extra sounds? Are any letters reversed such as writing *d* for *b* or a backward *s*.

- **To score a 4, the word must be phonetically correct.**

    In other words, if you would sound out the word, you would pronounce it correctly. There can be no missing sounds and no additional sounds. And every letter must face the correct direction.

Notice you are actually following the levels of phonemic awareness. You are looking at the beginning (*Level 1*), end (*Level 2*), and middle vowel spellings (*Level 3*). Then you look at whether all the sounds are represented (*Level 4*). You can determine the phonemic awareness level of a student from this test.

It takes some practice to learn how to score the test. Keep in mind that we are looking a score *range* rather than a *specific* score. When you have to make a judgment call, it will not affect the final outcome.

How to Score

Number of Points	Description
0	No sound is represented with a grapheme that makes the sound.
1	**1 sound is represented with a grapheme that says the sound.** • It must be the beginning sound, main vowel, or end sound.
2	**2 sounds are represented with a grapheme that says the sound.** It must be: • Beginning and end sounds are correct. OR • Beginning sound and main vowel sound are correct. OR • Main vowel sound and end sound are correct.
3	**3 or more sounds are represented with a grapheme that says the sound.** • These must be the beginning sound, end sound, and main vowel sound. Do not count the other sounds. • The main vowel (vowel of the accented syllable) must be correct although the choice of the grapheme representation may be incorrect such as *e* to represent *ee* or *ea*.
4	**All the sounds are represented with a grapheme that says the sound** although the correct spelling of the sound may not be used such as *sircl* for *circle*. • Spelled phonetically correct. • No sounds have been left out and no sounds have been added. • No reversal of letters such as *d/b*. A reversal knocks the score back to a score of 3.
5	**Correct spelling**

Example of scoring of 6th grade test

Word	Score	Explanation
picher (pitcher)	4	All sounds are represented although ch was used instead of tch. There are no extra sounds.
bellongging (belonging)	3	All the sounds are represented but the extra g provides an extra sound. The first g is a part of the grapheme ng and the second g says /j/.
quoston (question)	2	Beginning and end sounds are represented correctly. The main vowel is not correct.
poblicle (publicly)	1	Only the beginning sound is correct; the middle vowel is incorrect. The end sound is not correct because you would never pronounce le as ly.
inflatid (inflated)	3/4	This spelling is phonetically correct. Some may argue that the id, doesn't really represent an /ud/ sound. Then it only be a 3. It is a judgment call.
ofall (awful)	1/2	This word is tricky. The end sound is correct. The way the au is pronounced varies in different parts of our country. In some parts of the country, the short o and au are pronounced alike. Then the beginning sound would be correct. It would be a 1 or 2 depending on your accent.
coferm (confirm)	3	Beginning, end, and middle vowel are correct. The main vowel is actually /r/ spelled er but ir also says /r/. There is a missing sound.
sukus (circus)	2	Only beginning and end sounds are correct. The ir spelling of /r/ in this word acts as the middle "vowel" and it is not represented.
TOTAL POINTS	21 /40	Only eight words are scored. This would be about a score of about 53 on a full test of twenty words. This is a 6th grade student. Other anomalies would show up with the full test.

Developmental Spelling Test Analysis Record

Score: 53   Phonemic Awareness Level: 2 to 3

Skills	Yes	No	If no, explain
• Consistently hears the beginning sounds of words and is able to represent them	X		
• Consistently hears the end sounds in words and is able to represent them	X		Usually le instead of ly
• Consistently hears the middle vowel sounds in words and is able to represent them		X	Spelled e as o and u as o; didn't hear /r/
• No letters are reversed	X		
• No additional sounds are added to words		X	Added g, n
• No sounds are left out		X	Left out n; er instead of ir
• Knows how to spell all suffixes		X	ed; ly, ful
• Knows how to add all suffixes		X	ed; ly
• Knows how to spell all the graphemes		X	au; ir; tch; ti; ci
• Uses all the "Real Rules" of English		X	adding suffixes

General analysis of this student based on test

- Has phonemic awareness between Level 2 and Level 3. This student cannot consistently hear the middle vowel sounds and does not hear *all* of the sounds in many of the words.

- Hears *most* of the sounds in words but adds and deletes sounds as well as not hearing the middle sound.

- Knows the alphabet and sounds with single letter graphemes, but does not know some of the more advanced spellings such as *tch, ti, ci,* and *aw,*

- Does not recognize suffixes so does not know how to add them to words or spell them.

Analyzing the results of the DST

The Developmental Spelling Test reveals which sounds are difficult for students to hear and whether or not the student hears all of the sounds in words. It also shows the basic understanding of the spellings of the phonemes and the "Real Rules" of English. As you look at the scores for each word, ask yourself these questions.

- Do they hear the beginning sounds? End sounds? Middle vowel sounds?

- Do they hear all the sounds? Omit sounds? Add sounds?

- Can they hear the difference between voiced and unvoiced pairs? Examples of confusion would be writing *j* for *ch* or *p* for *b*.

- Which graphemes do they know? Which ones don't they know?

- Do they use letters for sounds (*q* for /cu /or r for /ar/)? Examples would be writing *qt* for *cute* or *cr* for *car*.

- Do they know how to add prefixes and suffixes?

- What fundamental rules do they not understand? For example, do they know how *e, i,* and *y* make the c say /s/, g say /j/, and the vowels long or do they know how to change the *y* to *i*?

- Have they written letters backwards, such as the *d, b,* or *s*?

- Are they trying to remember the word visually? The word may have letters in scrambled order, such as *otiment* for *ointment*.

- Were some of the words learned previously? If a student is making gross errors on words, but suddenly spells one or two words correctly, it is noticeable that the correct spelling came from memory and not from understanding word structure.

These questions can also be asked as part of ongoing assessment as you evaluate regular spelling tests, sentences, paragraphs, and stories that students write. You can observe what kind of errors students are making.

General Interpretation of Scores

Good Readers: Scores of 90 to 100

Test scores of 90 and over indicate that the student needs no intervention. We all make some mistakes in spelling. Good readers benefit from good instruction in comprehension and vocabulary. Ninety-nine percent of these students most likely read at grade level and above.

Fair Readers: Scores of 80 to 89

Test scores between 80 - 89 indicate weak skills that need to be addressed either through individual help or group activities. The lower the score the more weaknesses there are.

These students have some skill deficiencies and may or may not read at grade level. Some may read one or two grade levels below their grade. They have more vocabulary development than those with lower scores and may know how to decode.

Poor Readers: Scores of 51 to 79

Test scores below 80 indicate a need for individual or small group interventions. These students need phonemic awareness games and instruction in all of the graphemes. They will not be substantially helped by just reading more. Even traditional phonics instruction does not benefit them much because their phonemic awareness skills are so low.

Most remedial readers fall into this group. These students usually read two or more grade levels below their grade, with most not reading above the fourth-grade level. Their inability to decode may not be obvious because they have memorized so many words and have developed highly sophisticated compensation skills. The lack of skills may appear as "not liking to read," "poor fluency" or "the inability to comprehend much of what is read." Their vocabulary development has been grossly impaired through lack of reading.

Very Poor Readers: Scores 50 and Below

These students usually read at a low level, often at the kindergarten or first-grade level. Although they know all of their letters and sounds, they may confuse a few of the consonants, such as w or y. They often have difficulty with voiced and unvoiced pairs (/b/p/, /d/t/, /h/j/)

and letter reversals. They may need help in writing the letters of the alphabet. Vocabulary development has been grossly impaired through lack of reading.

Some of these students may have some type of cognitive delay or impairment and receive special services from their school. For this reason, they may need to learn the essential skills at a slower pace.

Phonemic Awareness Assessments

There are three phonemic awareness assessments that test Phonemic Awareness Levels 1-5. The assessments can be given to a small group of students or to an individual student. It is important to be able to see and record the results of each response of each student.

1. *The Phonemic Segmentation Assessment*

    This tests the ability of students to hear all of the sounds in a spoken word. It tests Level 4 of phonemic awareness.

    This assessment is difficult for struggling readers of all ages. Even high school students may put down only three or four chips for a word that has eight sounds. It readily identifies any weaknesses in phonemic awareness.

2. *The Phoneme Manipulation Assessment*

    This tests the ability of students to manipulate beginning, end, and middle sounds in spoken words. It tests Level 5 of phonemic awareness.

    Most older struggling readers can do fairly well on this test because of their knowledge of spelling. It identifies students with severe phonemic awareness weaknesses.

3. *The Sound Card Assessment*

    This tests the ability of students to hear the long and short vowel sounds in the middle of words. It tests Level 3 of phonemic awareness and the ability to connect the sound with the grapheme that represents the sound.

    You will be able to identify which long or short vowel sounds students have difficulty hearing. Most older struggling readers will do fairly well on this assessment.

Phoneme Segmentation Assessment

This is conducted in the same way as the Chip Game on page 65 except you *do not* help students make any corrections to the chips.

Materials: Each student has fifteen colored counting chips that are one color on one side and another color on the other. (You may also use chips of any two different colors.)

- "I will say a word and you will put down a chip for every sound you hear in the word. You will not be spelling the word but only putting a chip for every sound you hear.
- "The gray chips will be consonants. The white chips will be vowels.
- "What are vowels?" If the student has no idea, then tell them they can use any color they want.
- "If the sound is a consonant, put down a gray chip.
- "If the sound is a vowel, put down a white chip."

Procedure:

- Choose words from the correct level.

- Do the practice word before you start scoring. If students need help putting down the chips correctly, help them *with the practice word only*. This is to ensure they know what is required of them in the assessment.

- Say the word. Have the student put down the chips. Do not help them make any corrections.

- On the record sheet, put a slash through every incorrect chip. Ø

- Add a + sign at the end of the row if a student puts down more chips than sounds.

Phoneme Segmentation Record Sheet

Place a slash Ø through every chip that is incorrect. If a student puts down more chips than sounds, put a + sign after the row of chips.

 Level K   Use for Kindergarten and early Grade 1
 Level 1   Use for Grade 1 and early Grade 2
 Level 2   Use for Grade 2 through about Grade 4
 Level 3   Use for Grades 5 and up

Words			Chips
Practice	Level K	mat	● ○ ●
	Level 1	land	● ○ ● ●
	Level 2	little	● ○ ● ●
	Level 3	computer	● ○ ● ● ● ○ ● ●
	Level K	me	● ○
	Level 1	bent	● ○ ● ●
	Level 2	nicely	● ○ ● ● ○
	Level 3	perspective	● ● ● ● ○ ● ● ○ ●
	Level K	pet	● ○ ●
	Level 1	funny	● ○ ● ○
	Level 2	mismatched	● ○ ● ● ○ ● ●
	Level 3	motivation	● ○ ● ○ ● ○ ● ○
	Level K	home	● ○ ●
	Level 1	wiser	● ○ ● ●
	Level 2	unwisely	○ ● ● ○ ● ● ○
	Level 3	sophisticated	● ○ ● ○ ● ● ○ ● ○ ● ●
	Level K	plant	● ● ○ ● ●
	Level 1	platter	● ● ○ ● ●
	Level 2	flexible	● ● ○ ● ○ ● ●
	Level 3	proclamation	● ● ○ ● ● ○ ● ○ ● ○ ●

Phonemic Manipulation Assessment

- "You will use the chips again, but it does not matter what color you use. When I say a word, put down or change a chip for each sound."

○ = indicates the chip that is changed or inserted

Manipulating Beginning Sounds

Words	Chips	Question
sat	● ● ●	Put a chip down for every sound you hear in *sat*.
bat	○ ● ●	Which chip will you change if you change the word from *sat* to *bat*? Change it.
hat	○ ● ●	Which chip will you change if you change the word from *bat* to *hat*? Change it.

Manipulating End Sounds

pat	● ● ●	Put a chip down for every sound you hear in *pat*.
pass	● ● ○	Which chip will you change if you change the word from *pat* to *pass*? Change it.
pal	● ● ○	What chip will you change if you change the word from *pass* to *pal*? Change it.

Adding and Deleting Sounds

bet	● ● ●	Put down a chip for every sound you hear in *bet*.
bent	● ● ○ ●	How would you change *bet* to *bent*?
best	● ● ○ ●	How would you change *bent* to *best*?
test	○ ● ● ●	How would you change *best* to *test*?
tent	● ● ○ ●	How would you change *test* to *tent*?
ten	● ● ●	How would you change *tent* to *ten*?

Sound Card Assessment

<u>Materials</u>:

1 set cards with short vowel spellings a, e, i, o, u

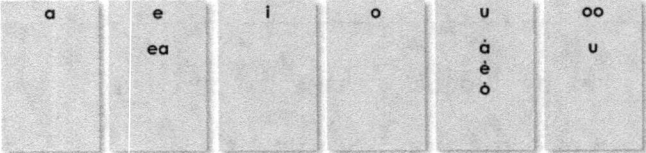

1 set cards with long vowel spellings a, e, i, o, u, oo

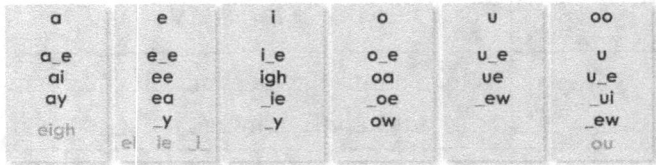

<u>Word Levels:</u>   Choose the correct level for your student.

Level 1 for Grades 1 – 4
Level 2 for Grades 5 and up

<u>Procedure:</u>

- Have students lay out the long vowel cards first.
- Choose the words appropriate for the grade: Level 1 or Level 2.
- Ask students to find the sound they hear in the middle of the word you say.
- Have students find the card, lift it under their chins, and say the sound.
- Put a slash through any word missed. Tally the errors.
- Then have students lay out the short vowel cards and find the sounds. Proceed in the same way.

Long Vowel Sound Card Record Sheet

- "Lay the long vowel Sound Cards out in a row on the table in front of you.
- "I will say a word. Find the card that shows the sound you hear in the middle of the word. Pick it up and place it under your chin to show me. Then say the sound you hear in the middle of the word."

- "What sound do you hear in the middle of _____?"

Put a slash through any word missed. Then circle the vowel.

Level 1: Grades 1- 4

	a	i	o	u
Level 1	rage	hiked	soaked	mules
	oo	**e**	**oo**	**e**
	flute	meter	spooned	stream
	o	**a**	**i**	**u**
	thrown	traded	smile	fumes

Level 2: Grades 5 and up

	a	i	o	u
Level 2	enabled	assigned	explode	amused
	oo	**e**	**oo**	**e**
	duty	pier	wound	seize
	o	**a**	**i**	**u**
	enrolled	weighty	exile	bugle

Short Vowel Sound Card Record Sheet

- "Lay the short vowel sound cards out in a row on the table in front of you."

- "What sound do you hear in the middle of _____?"

Put a slash through any word missed. Then circle the vowel.

Level 1: Grades 1-4

Level 1	i	e	i	a	o
	little	fetch	drink	sank	frog
	u	e	o	a	u
	must	pen	strong	plant	hung

Level 2: Grades 5 and up

Level 2	i	e	i	a	o
	fiddle	wreck	shrink	shrank	thought
	u	e	o	a	u
	thrust	breadth	frosty	platter	duster

Summary: Number of long and short vowels missed

Record the number missed for each vowel sound

	a	e	i	o	u	oo
Long vowels						
Short vowels						

Informal Reading Analysis

You need to know at what grade level the student is reading before your initial instruction. This can be determined through several means:

1. Assessments at school
2. Formal test such as the *Woodcock Reading Mastery Test* given by you or a specialist.
3. *Informal Reading Analysis* given by you using texts of predetermined reading levels such as those found in published informal reading inventories.

Your goal is to identify a text that a student can read which is at the instructional level. If you are a teacher, this assessment can be done in conjunction with Running Records.

Initial Assessment

The Informal Reading Analysis helps you identify the instructional reading level of the student as well as providing information on decoding skills, knowledge of graphemes, understanding of the "Real Rules" of English, and fluency.

1. **Instructional reading level of student**

   Identify the instructional reading level of students. If you use texts with predetermined reading levels, you will be able to find the grade level at which the student is reading. Use the guidelines of the informal reading inventory or the Five Finger rule of stopping to decode two to five words per one hundred.

2. **Decoding Skills**

   When students must stop to figure out a word, what strategy do they use? Do they guess or do they know how to break apart a word to decode it? How well can students decode both small and multisyllable words? Students need to break the habit of guessing.

3. **Knowledge of graphemes**

   How well do students know the graphemes? If this is a follow-up analysis, what graphemes are still problematic?

4. **Knowledge of the "Real Rules" of English**

   How well do students know the *"Real Rules" of English* such as realizing the markers make the vowel long or that markers after a *c* make it say /s/ ands the *g* say /j/?

5. **Fluency**

   How smoothly do students read? Do they read in phrases? Do they pay attention to punctuation? Do they read with expression? Use the *Oral Reading Fluency Rubric* to score fluency.

Oral Reading Fluency Rubric

1	Reads at a labored, slow pace. Reads word by word with a lack of intonation and expression. May have numerous pauses or repetitions. Some words are not read correctly.
2	Reads mostly in a slow, choppy manner but sometimes reads in two and three word phrases. Has some difficulty with punctuation signals to pause or change voice. Some words are not read correctly. Does not read with expression.
3	Reads at a reasonable pace and is mostly smooth but has poor phrasing and intonation. There may be some choppiness and possible repetitions, and/or may read right through punctuation as if it were not there. Uses some expression or changes voice when reading.
4	Reads smoothly at a reasonable place with good expression and intonation. Knows how to pause or change voice with punctuation.

Informal Reading Analysis Summary

1. Oral Reading Fluency Score _____

2. Estimated reading grade level _____

3. Decodes unknown words rather than guesses   YES   SOME   NO

4. Knows how to decode small words   YES   SOME   NO

5. Knows how to decode multisyllable words   YES   SOME   NO

6. Keeps place in text while reading   YES   SOME   NO

Identify the errors. Write the errors in the box below the spellings. Have you taught these yet?

Long vowel spellings	Short vowel spellings	oi/oy	ou/ow	au/aw augh
c says /s/ ce, ci, cy	g says /j/ ge, gi, gy, dge	kn, gn	wr, ir, ur, er ear	nk/ng
sh = ti, si, ci	How markers work	Which Suffixes	Which Prefixes	

Ongoing formative assessment

The Phoneme Segmentation (Chip Game), the Phoneme Manipulation, The Sound Cards (Sound Card Game), and the Informal Reading Analysis can all be used as ongoing monitoring tools. The scoring principles of the Developmental Spelling Test can be used to assess student writing and spelling. These games and assessments will provide continual feedback on student progress.

As you listen to students read, use the lens of the Informal Reading Analysis to determine how students are progressing and what skills are still missing. They should be steadily progressing in their reading levels, ability to decode, understanding of graphemes and the "Real Rules" of English (see Appendix C), and fluency.

If students are unable to decode a word, is it because they have not learned the grapheme and the "Real Rules" that govern it OR is it because they still do not know how to decode? If it is just because they do not know the grapheme, you can tell them and know they will eventually learn it in the lessons. If it is a decoding problem, then stop and again show them how to break a word apart.

Students must ALWAYS be reading at the instructional level. As you teach the lessons, students can progress fairly rapidly. I've had students progress one grade level in six lessons. Every few lessons have them read two or three minutes in the text they are using. You will quickly be able to determine if they are reading at the appropriate level.

Chapter 17:
Special Situations

Become a keen observer of students.
Become tuned to their needs.

Carefully observe the behaviors and responses of students as you teach. It will help you fine-tune your teaching. Perhaps, you just have to adjust the pace of the lessons. Some students need to progress more slowly than normal and some need to progress more quickly. April from Chapter One learned so quickly that we did two lessons in one. At the other end of the spectrum, Jakob needed more time than usual. But both learned to read well.

Becoming an attentive observer will also alert you to needs that must be addressed by another professional. Teaching the right content in the right sequence with the right instruction will help most students learn to read, even those with learning disabilities, speech impairments, autistic spectrum, and other physical disabilities. Some learners, though, may need extra attention.

English Language Learners

Phonemic awareness is a foundation skill for learning to read. If students have phonemic awareness in their own language, then it is easier for them to listen for the speech sounds in English. Those who cannot hear the speech sounds in their native language will also have difficulty hearing the sounds in English. The right instruction will help them gain phonemic awareness.

English language learners will also need to learn speech sounds that are found in our language but not in their native language. That may require extra work with sound cards with those particular phonemes.

English Language Learners in a first grade classroom

In a school with 77 percent of the students on free or reduced lunch and 55 percent white and 45 percent black, Hispanic, and multiracial, it was common for nearly all students in first grade to leave the classroom reading *below* grade level. In the year of our research, first grade students were placed in classrooms according to their ability. The lowest ability classroom had students who began the school year reading *below* pre-kindergarten level to beginning kindergarten level. Two of these were English language learners who spoke no English. The goal for this classroom was to achieve three-fourths grade level by the end of first grade.

The school had a transient population with many children remaining in class for a only a few months. For that reason, only 8 out of 20 students attended the full year and can be reported with accuracy. Other students who had significant gains cannot be reported because they did not attend the full year.

The teacher implemented the right content in the right sequence with the right instruction. The results? All achieved higher than expected. Rather than achieving the goal of three-fourths of a grade level, each of these students gained more than two grade levels, including the English Language Learners. The grade-level equivalence levels shown on the chart are those recommended by Fountas & Pinnell.

- Five left first grade reading at grade level.
- All students gained two grade levels in one year,

All of these students gained more than two years within one school year.

ELL — English Language Learner, student who could not speak English

☐ Gains from beginning of year to end of year reading levels

Student	below Pre-k	Pre-K	Kindergarten				Grade1					
	↓aa	aa	A	B	C	D	E	F	G	H	I	J
1												
2												
3												
4												
5 ELL												
6 ELL												
7												
8												

Hearing impaired

Students may have a hearing impairment that has not been recognized because they have passed hearing screenings at school. They often do not hear all of the sounds in spoken words. The words "good night" might be heard only as "ood ight." These students do not have phonemic awareness because of their inability to hear the sounds. How will you know when to recommend the student see a specialist?

- Students leave out sounds when they speak. They may leave off the beginning sounds and/or the end sounds in words.

- The phonemic awareness games are difficult for them to complete successfully. They may refuse to do them or become agitated when asked to play them.

- They don't respond to you unless you are facing them.

- They may often ask, "What?"

Sheri

Sheri was a bright, happy child in my first grade classroom. Her speech pattern was unusual, but I didn't think too much about it at first. When she spoke, she didn't say the beginning sounds of many words. However, I noticed that she did not always respond to questions, and the sound card games were difficult for her. I began to suspect some kind of hearing impairment. I placed her in the front row right in front of me so I could be near her and face her. She left first grade reading well.

She had passed the hearing screening at school, but I still recommended having her hearing checked. The summer between her first and second grade those tests were finally done. Doctors found that she had significant hearing loss and depended largely on lip-reading. She had been successful in my classroom because I had learned to be near her and face her. Unfortunately, her type of hearing loss could not be treated with any kind of hearing aid. However, to be successful in school, her teachers and parents needed to know about her disability and how to accommodate her.

Vision impairments

We are aware of obvious vision problems when students squint to see something in the distance or hold the book too close because they cannot see well. But some impairments are not as obvious. Students can pass a standard vision test with 20/20 vision and yet have significant visual deficiencies. They often have difficulty learning to read and when they do learn to read well with the right instruction, they still have problems reading and comprehending. The following are the most common undetected vision problems:

1. Delayed or incomplete vision development
2. Eye-teaming and focusing problems
3. Eye movement control and tracking problems
4. Lazy eye and wandering eye.

Many time students don't complain because they assume what they experience with their vision is normal. They don't know why they can't understand the text or why it is confusing. If they do complain, it is usually not about their vision but about how difficult it is for them to understand what they have read or how much they don't like to read. In reality, one or more of these might be the real problem:

- Their eyes blur when changing from distance to near such as looking at a screen or whiteboard at the front of the room to their book or notes. Their eyes do not refocus quickly.

- They have double vision but they think it is normal.

- One eye shuts down so they miss letters, words, phrases, or chunks of paragraphs.

- Their eyes don't focus and refocus quickly so they lose their place and skip words or even whole lines.

- One eye might focus on one word while the other eye looks at another word. Their eyes are not working together. But the student may not realize it. These students just know the text is confusing.

How do you detect a potential problem? Here are some of the behaviors that may indicate a vision problem.

- Avoids reading reading whenever possible. They may appear to be unmotivated or inattentive.

- Decodes words with great difficulty despite being taught how to decode.

- Easily loses the line of text while reading and may even skip lines.

- Tilts head or covers one eye when reading.
- Reads laboriously word by word, pointing at each word or even each letter.
- Rapidly tires when reading even when it is within their attention span.
- Avoids near, visually demanding tasks by avoiding reading or by constantly looking away from a text.
- Has difficulty copying text from whiteboard, chalkboard, or screen.
- Confuses t's and l's, misses letters in a word, or reverses letters in a word.
- Complains of print being unstable.
- Complains of double vision or blurred vision.

Fortunately, most of these issues can be corrected through vision therapy by a behavioral vision specialist.

Brittany

Brittany was in third grade when I started working with her. She did not have phonemic awareness and had no idea how the sounds were represented in speech. She was barely reading at a primer level. After just a few lessons, she gained phonemic awareness and understood how to build words. She could hardly wait to learn the next grapheme.

However, even though she learned to decode, her reading was laborious, slow, and seemed to require her to stop and look at every single letter in the word. She had to "sound out" every word even though she knew the graphemes and sounds. Nothing seemed to correct the problem.

One day she walked into the room and said, "I know what we are going to do today! We are going to use the *ur* spelling." She spied the list of words on the table and while just glancing at them, she rattled them off: "*nurse, purse, church...*" We started the lesson and after spelling the words, she took the list and began reading. "/n/..../ur/..../se/" She could hardly read the words.

I knew then that there was some other issue. And there was. When a specialist tested her eyes, he found she had a vision impairment that prevented her from being able to track a line of text. When she received vision therapy from a specialist, she soared. She graduated salutatorian of her high school graduating class.

Daniel

Daniel was in second grade and was generally a good student. However, I noticed something strange about his behavior. He would look down at his work for only a few seconds and then would look away at a distance. Up and down. Up and down. He had classic behavior for a student who had focusing problems. When I asked his parents about any vision issues, they said he had a "lazy eye" as a child, but that was corrected. They took him to a specialist and discovered he had a vision impairment that required specialized care. When he received vision therapy, he was then able to read without interruption.

Intellectual disability

In working with students with a wide range of abilities and disabilities, I have found that almost all students can learn to read well. The exception would be a student with a diagnosis of intellectual disability. If a student has an IQ below 70, learning to decode may not be possible. I had such a student who developed phonemic awareness, learned the simple graphemes, and the ability to build words, but could not read what he had written. Researchers have also found that these students hit a wall when it comes to decoding. Instead, with the foundation, they can memorize some words that help them in daily life.

The challenge is to teach the right content in the right sequence with the right instruction. Students that may seem hopeless may not be. Remember the second grade student that specialists had declared incapable of learning "letters and sounds?" With the right content taught in the right sequence with the right instruction, she was reading at grade level by the end of the year. Give all students in your care a chance to learn to read. Almost all of them will be able to become proficient readers. I

In Summary

1. Teaching the right content in the right sequence with the right instruction will help almost all students learn to read,

2. English Language Learners need to learn the phonemes of English.
   - English will have phonemes that differ from their native language.
   - ELL students who have phonemic awareness in their own language do better than those who do not.

3. Some hearing impairments may go undetected with normal hearing screenings.
   - Hearing impaired students have difficulty hearing the sounds in words.
   - With compensations, they can learn to read well.

4. Some vision impairments go undetected with normal vision tests
   - Vision impairments hinder the ability to attend to reading even when students have the foundational skills.
   - Vision impairments require a behavioral vision specialist.

5. Students will intellectual disabilities with IQ's below 70 are limited in their ability to learn to read.
   - They may be able to gain alphabet knowledge and phonemic awareness.
   - They may not be able to learn how to decode words.

Chapter 18:
The Plan

**Change a life.
Give the gift of reading.**

What do students need, especially those who struggle? They need the right content taught in the right sequence with the right instruction.

The Right Instruction	• Errorless learning and immediate feedback • Confidence that students can achieve • Kinesthetic strategies for every concept.
The Right Content	• Hear the individual sounds in spoken words • Know the spellings of the 42-44 speech sounds • Put sounds and spellings together to form words • Know how to add prefixes and suffixes • Be able to decode small and big words • Read smoothly with expression • Think about meaning
The Right Sequence	• The sequence the brain uses in processing words

What you need to do

1. Assess the student before initial instruction.

Know what skills the student has and does not have. The essential assessments are found in Chapter 16. You need to know:

- The reading grade level.
- The phonemic awareness level.
- The Developmental Spelling test score.
- What graphemes, prefixes, and suffixes are a problem as seen in the Developmental Spelling test.
- What long and short vowel sounds are a problem.
- If the student is young or an English Language Learner, what alphabet letters are not known.

Once you start instruction, the phonemic awareness games, word building, and reading will be ongoing assessments used to monitor the progress of students. You will have continual feedback on what the student knows and does not know.

SPECIAL NOTE: The Developmental Spelling Test can be used as a screening tool for an entire classroom or school. The test can be given as a regular spelling test, but the words are scored using the 0-5 point scale for each word. This test will identify students that are at risk and those who need extra help. Teachers can use this test at the beginning of the year to identify students who will need extra help.

2. **Play phonemic awareness games.**

    Develop the phonemic awareness skills of your students. You want them to reach Level 6. The Chip game, Sound Card game, and word building will help students reach this level. Students need to be able to:

    - Hear and manipulate the individual sounds in spoken words.
    - Identify the grapheme that represents each sound.

3. **Review the graphemes taught.**

    In every lesson, take two to five minutes to review the last graphemes taught or ones that are still a problem.

4. **Teach new graphemes and the "Real Rules."**

    The graphemes for the 43 sounds and the "Real Rules" of English are found in the Appendices.

5. **Engage students in word building on the whiteboard.**

    Choose words that use the new graphemes. For example, if you are teaching the graphemes *oi* and *oy*, you will want to use words like the following. Give the base word and then have the student change it by adding suffixes and prefixes.

oi	oy
oil, oiling	joy, enjoy, enjoyment
boil boiling, boiled	annoy, annoying
noise, noisy	destroy, destroyer
choice	employ, employer, employed, unemployed

6. **Teach decoding.**

    Some students will need to be taught now to decode small words. All have to be taught how to decode multisyllable words.

7. **Have students read the words they have built.**

    Students *must* read the words they spell on the whiteboard. They must have digital or paper access to these words so they can read and reread them. This is where they apply their knowledge of graphemes and practice their decoding skills.

8. **Have students read challenge words.**

    Students *must* use their decoding skills to read unknown, multisyllable words. In a lesson on *oi* and *oy*, older students might read words like *boisterous, deployment,* or *unavoidable.* They must have practice tackling these big words in order to be independent readers.

9. **Review student reading logs.**

    Track how much students are reading and how many words are difficult. This will help you know if the reading level is correct, and if students are reading 30 minutes per day, five days a week. They cannot become proficient readers if they are not reading a sufficient amount of time at their instructional level.

10. **Check reading level of chosen book.**

    Periodically have students read to you. This does not have to be every lesson, but if you suspect a book is too easy, it is important to listen to students read for one to two minutes.

11. **Assign writing based on the text students are reading.**

    Choose an appropriate writing assignment. This is a critical element that builds reading comprehension. Writing requires the ability to pull information out of a text, to understand sentence structure, and to know correct spelling and punctuation. Model the writing assignment, have students write, and have them edit their piece and correct the errors.

12. **Have students revise and edit the writing assignment.**

    When students bring the written composition at the next lesson, help students further revise and edit the assignment so it is written correctly. *Let the pen stay in the hand of the student.*

A special note on cross-lateral exercise

Recent research has demonstrated that cross-lateral movement, any movement where the arm crosses the midsection of the body, stimulates learning in the brain. It causes the two sides of the brain to communicate with each other. In this approach to teaching reading, cross-lateral exercise is built-into the following activities:

- Writing on the whiteboard if it requires students to reach across the mid-body.
- The Chip game
- The Sound card game
- Writing in the air
- Acting out the sound
- Kinesthetic decoding

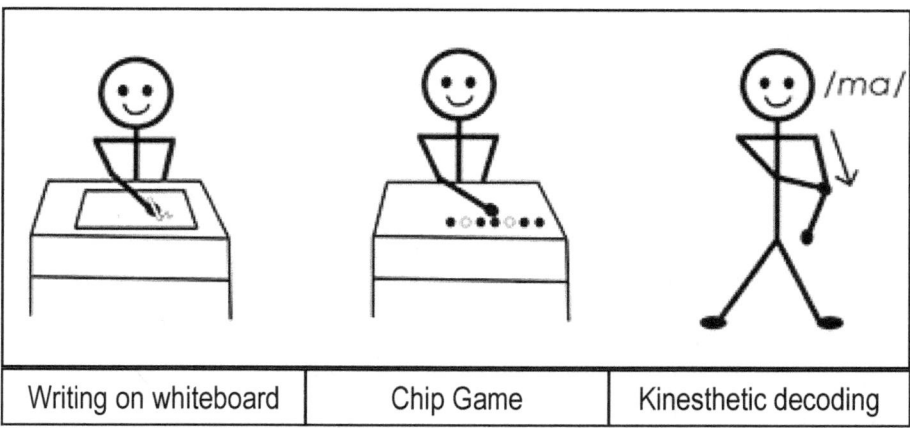

| Writing on whiteboard | Chip Game | Kinesthetic decoding |

You have the tools

You have in your hands the tools to help every student become proficient in reading. You are the one who can provide a solid foundation for young beginning readers so they never have to struggle. You are the one who can make the difference in the lives of struggling readers. With practice, you can become skilled with each strategy. *The "Real Rules" of English"* and the *Roxie Reading*™ curriculum series are resources that provide invaluable details. You may feel unsure at first, but you will still see results because the principles work. The research is correct.

Believe students can achieve, never giving up hope on any student. Almost all students can learn to read well if they are taught the right content in the right sequence with the right instruction.

Appendix A:
The Graphemes for the Speech Sounds

Graphemes for the 43 Sounds

Here are the 43 sounds of English along with the most common ways to spell the sound. An example word is given for each spelling. Some spellings are used in many words; some are used in only a few words. The more unusual spellings are listed last.

Short Vowels	a	bat	e ea	let bread	i _y_	fit system
	o ough	hot thought	u a e o ou	hut was the other touch	oo u ou	foot put could
Long Vowels	a a_e ai ay eigh ei	acorn sale pail play eight reins	e e_e ee ea y ie ei i ey	me even seed seat baby chief receive radio honey	i i_e igh y ie	wild like light fry pie
	o o_e oa ow _oe ough ou	bold mole boat show toe though shoulder	u u_e ew _ue eu	human mule few argue feud	oō u_e _ew _ue u ui o_e o ou ough	moon ruler flew blue truth fruit move do you through
Consonants	b	bat	c k ck ch que	cat kite pick school antique	d	dog

Consonants

f	funny	g	goat	h	hat
ph	photo	gu	guide		
gh	tough				
j	jar	l	late	m	mother
g(e)	gem			mb	lamb
g(i)	giant			mn	column
g(y)	gym				
dge	edge				
n	none	p	pan	qu	queen
kn	know				
gn	sign				
pn	pneumonia				
r	road	s	sun	t	table
er	her	c(e)	face		
ir	shirt	c(i)	cinder		
ur	hurt	c(y)	cycle		
wr	write	ps	psychology		
ear	learn				
rh	rhyme				
our	journal				
yr	zephyr				
or	sailor				
ar	collar				
v	vase	w	water	x	exit
y	yellow	z	zoo	_s_	usual
		_s	has		
		x	xylophone		

Other Consonants

th	thin	th	those	wh	while
sh	shine	ch	chain	ng	thing
ti	nation	tch	catch	_n_	bank
si	mission				
ci	musicians				
ch	chef				

Other Vowels	oi oy	boil boy	ou ow ough	couch town bough	ar	star
	a au aw augh	salt sauce lawn daughter				
Special Patterns	war	warm	wor	world	_ture	nature
	_ain	curtain	_ous	fabulous	_sure	treasure

Appendix B: Actions for the Sounds

Acting out the sound is one of the most powerful strategies you can use. For some students, this activity alone makes the difference between reading failure and reading success. Students act out the speech sound that an object or action *makes*.

Grapheme	Action	Instructions
short a	say /ă/ when scared	Let's pretend we just saw a mouse. Let's throw our hands up and say /ă/.
b	beating heart	/b/ reminds me of a beating heart. Let's pretend we are beating hearts and say the sound /b/. (Take the right fist and beat in rhythm against the heart.)
c	camera - click	/c/ reminds me of taking a picture with a camera (or phone). When I push the button to take the picture, it says /c/. (Pretend to hold a camera to take a picture. Pretend to push the button and say /c/.)
d	shoe in washing machine	/d/ sounds like a tennis shoe in a washing machine, hitting the sides of the washer as it is washing. (Make a wide circle with one arm (the tub of the washing machine). Make a fist with the other hand and make a circular motion inside the tub, hitting the side of the washer with a jerk and saying /d/ as it "hits" the side.)
short e	Grandpa can't hear	/ĕ/ reminds me of what a grandpa might say if he can't hear you. Let's put a hand to our ears and say /ĕ/? (Cup one hand around one ear, turn your head a little, and lean forward as if you are trying to hear someone speak.)
f	flying with wings	The /f/ sound reminds me of the sound of wings of a bird as they are flying through the air. (Flap your arms like you are flying. It is the sound of the wings whooshing through the air that makes the /f/ sound.)

Grapheme	Action	Instructions
g	drinking water - gulping	If I am drinking a glass of water fast, sometimes it sounds like /g/. Let's pretend we are drinking water and say /g/. (Pretend to hold a glass up to your mouth and be gulping down the water. /g//g/g/g/g/g/g/.)
h	out of breath running	/h/ sounds like a runner out of breath after running a long way. Let's pretend we have just finished a long, hard race and say /h/. (Pretend like you are running with your arms moving at your side and saying /h/.)
short i	gross or nasty -- icky, sticky goo	If we were pulling up icky, sticky goo from our hands, we would say /ĭ/. (Hold one palm out with pretend nasty, gross, icky, goo on it and with the other hand, pretend you are pulling up the goo and saying /ĭ/.)
j	jumping rope	/j/ reminds me of jumping rope. It is the sound of the rope hitting the ground. (Go through the actions of jumping rope and say /j/ as the rope would hit the ground.)
k	camera - click	(Same as /c/)
l	beaters on a mixer	/l/ reminds me of an electric mixer, making a cake. Let's pretend we are mixers and say the sound /l/. (Move your fist around in a small, fast circular motion and say /l/. If students are not aware of the sound of an electric mixer, you may have to bring in one and have them "hum" the /l/ with the sound of the motor.)

Grapheme	Action	Instructions
m	good taste - rub tummy	/m/ reminds me of what we say when we eat something good. What is your favorite food? Say /m/ and rub our tummies as we say the sound /m/.
n	race car driver	/n/ reminds me of a race car driver. Pretend you are driving a car and say /n/. (Pretend you are gripping the steering wheel of a race car and driving.)
short o	open mouth for doctor	/ŏ/ reminds me of opening my mouth when a doctor wants to look in my throat. Let's pretend we have to say /ŏ/ for the doctor. (Use your index finger as the tongue depressor, open your mouth and point your finger to your open mouth -- don't touch it -- and say /o/.)
p	popcorn popping	/p/ reminds me of popcorn popping. Let's pretend that popcorn is popping and say /p/. (Flick the fingers of both hands quickly in the air and say /p/p/p/p/p/ as if popcorn were popping.)
q	duck quacking	If you say the /qu/ (sounds like /kw) very fast it sounds like a duck quacking. Let's pretend we are quacking ducks. (Put your thumb and fingers together to form a duck's beak. Move them together and apart to look like a duck quacking.)
r	scary growl of dog (or lion)	/r/ sounds like a growling lion. Let's pretend we are lions growling and say /r/.

Grapheme	Action	Instructions
s	snake hissing	/s/ sounds like a snake hissing. Say /s/ as you pretend to be a snake slithering through the grass. (Extend both arms with palms together and make a slithering motion.)
t	lawn sprinkler	/t/ reminds me of a sprinkler that makes the /t/ sound as it moves in a circle. Let's pretend we are sprinklers and say /t/. . . /t/. . . /t/. (Extend the right arm straight out to the side. In a jerking motion, move the arm across the front of the body to the left shoulder, forming a semi-circle. Say /t/ at each jerky motion.)
short u	don't know something	Sometimes I say /ŭ/ when I don't know the answer. I am trying to make up my mind and decide what to do. Do you want a cookie or a piece of cake? (Put your finger to your cheek and look like you don't know the answer as you say /u/.)
v	cell phone vibration	The /v/ sound reminds me of a cell phone that is vibrating. Let's pretend we have a cell phone and say /v/. (Pretend like you have a cell phone in your pocket and it is vibrating. Clutch your hand over your pocket and make it vibrate.)
w	rodeo rope	/w/ reminds me of a cowboy twirling a rope over his or her head. Let's pretend we are cowboys twirling ropes and say the sound /w/. (Twirl imaginary rope above head and say /w/.)
x	open a soda (pop) can	/x/ reminds me opening a can of pop that has been shaken up. Let's pretend to open a can of pop and say /x/. (Hold an imaginary pop can in one hand and as you pretend to open it, say /x/.)

Grapheme	Action	Instructions
y	karate chop	/y/ reminds me of a karate chop. (Take a karate stance with one hand vertical, palm flat and the other hand horizontal, palm down. Then do the chop by moving the horizontal hand quickly away from you.)
z	buzzing bee	/z/ sounds like a buzzing bee. Say /z/ as you pretend to be a bee buzzing around. (Hold your thumb and index finger together and you make zigzag motions and say /z/.)
Long a	agree	If we like something and agree with it, we can say /ay/! (Lift both arms, bent at elbow with thumbs up in the air. Give a strong thumbs up.)
Long e	scared	We might make the /ee/ sound if we see a mouse run across the room in front of us. (Have students draw backward and draw their arms and hands to their bodies like they just saw a mouse and say /ee/.)
Long i	sailor saluting	The sound reminds me of a sailor who is saluting an officer and says "aye, aye." (Stand at attention, salute, and say "aye, aye.")
Long o	something bad	Sometimes when something happens that I didn't want to happen, I might say "oh! oh!" (Pretend something happened that you did not want to happen. Hit both cheeks with the palms of your hand and say 'oh, oh.")

Grapheme	Action	Instructions
Long u	smelly	Pretend you smell a skunk. Hold your nose and say "u_e." (Hold your nose and emphatically say /u_e/.)
th	angry goose	/th/ sounds like an angry goose.(Flap elbows like wings and say /th/.)
th (voiced)	swarm of bees	The voiced /th/ sounds like a swarm of bees. Move open hands, fingers apart in arbitrary motions to look like a swarm of bees.
sh	quiet	/sh/ reminds me to be very quiet. Let's pretend to tell everyone to be quiet and say /sh/. Put your forefinger to lips as you say /sh/.
ch	train	/ch/ reminds me of engine of a train going down the tracks. Let's pretend we are trains and say /ch/. (Move arms at your side like the wheels on a train engine.)
wh	blowing out candle	/wh/ reminds me of blowing out a candle. Let's pretend we are blowing out a candle and say /wh/. (Lean forward and pretend to blow out candles on a birthday cake.)
ng	hitting gong	/ng/ reminds me of the sound made when someone hits a big gong. Let's pretend to hit a gong and say the sound /ng/. (Pretend to hit a gong by making a striking motion with your hand.)
oo	owl	Let's pretend we are owls and turn our heads completely to the right and then to the left and say /oo/. (Be very still except turn your head completely to the right and completely to the left as you say /oo/.)

Grapheme	Action	Instructions
ar	pirate	/ar/ reminds me of a pirate who says /ar/. Let's pretend we are pirates and say /ar/. (Swing the arm in front of the body, cover your eye with the other hand, and scrunch up your face as you say /ar/.)
ou	hurt	We say /ow/ when we are hurt. Let's pretend we just touched a hot stove with our finger. (Pretend you have just touched a hot stove with your finger and quickly lift your finger from the stove and say /ow/.)
aw	pencil broke	Let's pretend our pencil just broke and we say /au/. We say /au/ when something happens that we do not like such as having your pencil break in half. (Make the motion of your pencil breaking into two pieces and say /aw/.)
oi	sea lion	Let's pretend we are sea lions slapping our flippers on the water and say /oi/. (Pretend like you are a sea lion, with your arms extended straight in front of you, palms horizontal to the floor. Clap your hands like the flippers hitting the water or ground.)
short oo	lift weights	Let's pretend we are lifting weights over our heads that are almost too heavy for us. We say /oo/ as we struggle to lift it. (Pretend like you are lifting a heavy barbell starting at waist position and lifting it with difficulty over your head. Say the sound /oo/ very slowly like it is almost too heavy to lift.)
_s_ (as in Asia)	saw	Let's pretend we are sawing wood and make the /_s_/ sound as we saw. (Use long arms motions, pretending to saw a huge piece of wood.)

Appendix C: The "Real Rules" of English

The "Real Rules" of English ™

Notice the importance of the markers e, i, and y.

The Markers e, i, y

- The letters *e*, *i*, and *y* are markers in our language. The markers make:
    1. A vowel say its own name.
       Examples are *side, shady, making*.
    2. The *c* say /s/.
       The marker must immediately follow the letter *c*.
       Examples are *ice, icy, icing*.
    3. The *g* say /j/.
       The marker must immediately follow the letter *g*.
       Examples are *age, gym, gem, giant*.

- You only need one marker so when adding a suffix, <u>throw away</u> the extra marker.
  Examples are *shade + ing = shading*.

- You can stop a marker by doubling the consonant or adding another consonant.
  Examples are *hopping, picnicking, little, badge*.

- An *l* is so skinny it does **not** stop the marker from working. You need another consonant.
  Examples are *table, idle*.

- A *v* can stop a marker all by itself.
  Examples are *have, live*.

The letter y

- *y* says /i/ at the end of a "one part word" (one syllable word).
  Examples are *my, fly, try*.

- *y* usually says /e/ at the end of a word with more than one syllable.
  Examples are *baby, lady, responsibility, emergency*.

- *y* is the most common way to spell the sound /ee/ at the end of a word.

- Change these *y*'s to *i* before adding all endings except *_ing*.
  Examples are *cry + ed = cried* and *cry + ing = crying*.

The letter v	• *v* never comes at the end of an English word. There is usually an *e* after it. • *v* is never doubled. An exception is *savvy*. • *v* can stop a marker all by itself. Examples are *love, have, give*.
Spellings that come only after a short vowel	• *_tch, _dge, _x,* and *_ck* come only after a short vowel. • The common exceptions are *such, much, rich, which, attach,* and *sandwich*. The less common exceptions are *bachelor, ostrich,* and *yak*. By the time young or remedial readers have read and spelled these words, these will not be a problem.
"uh" vowels and the schwa	• All vowels can say /uh/. Some examples are the words *hut, some, other, away,* and *the*. • Also note, in a two or more syllable word, the vowel in the unstressed syllable may say /uh/ or may not be pronounced clearly. This /uh/ sound, or unclear sound, can be indicated by a dot over the vowel to help students remember to pronounce the vowel /uh/. Some examples of /uh/ in the unstressed syllable are *dent<u>ist</u>, respons<u>ible</u>,* and *jack<u>et</u>*.
Compound words	• Compound words are two words put together without any changes to either word. Examples are *bookkeeper, sidewalk,* and *raincoat*.
/sh/	• /sh/ is spelled *sh, ti, ci, si,* and sometimes *ch*. • The most common way to spell /sh/ is *_ti*.
Adding prefixes	• Almost all prefixes are added directly to the word. • The exception are some Latin prefixes such as *in_* and *ad_*. The second letter is often changed to match the beginning letter of the word. Examples are *in + mature = i**m**mature* and *ad + prove = a**p**prove*. • A prefix can be added to a prefix.

Adding suffixes	• Five ways to add a suffix:
	  1. Just add the suffix without changing anything.
	     An example is *jump + ed = jumped*.
	  2. If the *word* **ends** in a marker, throw away the extra marker.
	     An example is *rake + ing =raking*.
	  3. If the *suffix* **begins** with a marker, double the consonant to keep the vowel short.
	     An example is *shop + ing = shopping*.
	  4. If the word ends in the grapheme y, change the y to i for all suffixes except *_ing*.
	     Examples are *try + ed = tried* and *try + ing = trying*.
	  5. If the suffix **begins** with *a* or *o*, *drop the e in words ending in e*.
	     An *e*xample is *pleasure + able = pleasurable*.
	     Keep the marker if you need it to make the vowel long, the g say /j/ or the c say /s/.
	     Examples are *knowledge + able = knowledgeable* and *notice + able = noticeable*.
	• A suffix can be added to a suffix.
	  An example is *depart + ment + al + ly = departmentally*.

/l/ at the end	• The most common way to spell the sound /l/ at the end of a two or more syllable word is *_le*. Only a few end in *_el*. • The way to spell the <u>suffix</u> /l/ is *_al* as in the word *departmental*.
able or __ible	• Usually use *_able*. If the word ends in *e*, throw the *e* away before adding *_able* unless the *e* is necessary as a marker. • Usually use *_ible* after the sounds /s/ or/j/.
__ant/__ance __ent/__ence	• Use *_ent* after the sounds /s/ and /j/. • Change *_ant* to *_ance* or *_ent* to *_ence* by <u>throwing away</u> the *t* and adding *_ce*. Examples are *silent* to *silence* and *important* to *importance*. • Change *_ant* to *_ancy* or *_ent* to *_ency* by <u>throwing away the</u> <u>t</u> and adding *_cy*. An example is *relevant* to *relevancy*.

_ed	• When _ed is added to the end of a word, it can say /t/, /d/, or /ud/. Examples are *marched* (/t/), *changed* (/d/), and *parted* (/ud/).
ou/ow **au/aw**	• Use *ou* in the middle of a word and *ow* at the end, except use *ow* in the middle when followed by a final *l* or *n* as in *owl* or *brown*. • Use *au* in the middle of a word and *aw* at the end, except use *aw* in the middle when followed by a final *l* or *n* as in *lawn* or *crawl*.
Ways to spell /r/	There are more ways to spell the sound /r/ than any other sound in our language. • *er* is the spelling of /r/ that usually comes at the end of a word with two or more syllables. It can be part of a word or added to a word. Examples are the words *hammer, anger,* and *swimmer*. • *wr* and *rh* come at the beginning as in *write* and *rhombus*. • *r, er, ir, ur* and *ear* can come at the beginning or in the middle. • *or, ar, yr,* and *our* are spellings that come at the end or in the middle of a few words such as in *collar, doctor, zephyr,* and *adjourn*.
Ways to spell /c/	• *c* is the beginning spelling. • *k* is the end and middle spelling of /k/, but is used at the beginning if the *c* would be followed by a marker *e, i,* or *y*. To prevent the *c* from saying /s/, the *k* is used such as in *kitchen* and *kind*. • *ck* comes only after a short vowel. The *k* stops the marker from working. This makes these words "marker ready." • *ch* is a spelling of /k/ that is used in a few words such as *school* and *Christmas*. • *_que* is a spelling of /k/ that is used in a few words such as in *unique* and *technique*.

Voiced and unvoiced pairs

- There are some consonants that students confuse, particularly those students who do not have good phonemic awareness skills or those who are just learning English. These consonant pairs are formed in the mouth in the same way, but one sound is voiced (uses the voice box) and the other sound is not.

Unvoiced	Voiced	Unvoiced example	Voiced example
/p/	/b/	poor	bore
/s/	/z/	loose	lose
/f/	/v/	file	vile
/th/	/th/	thin	then
/t/	/d/	to	do
/ch/	/j/	cheer	jeer
/k/	/g/	cold	gold
/sh/	/zh/	mission	vision
/wh/	/w/	whale	wait

Appendix D:
Answers

Horse

Phoneme Segmentation

Ηορσε

The horσε is ρυννινγ. The horσε wαντs to go hoμε.

This horσε βελονγσ to a yoυνγ girl thατ λιϖεσ δoων the στρεετ φροµ my γρανδµοτηερ. This horσε is a Σπανιση σταλλιον.

Here is the story.

Horse

The horse is running. The horse wants to go home.

This horse belongs to a young girl that lives down the street from my **grandmother**. This horse is a **Spanish** stallion.

Usually the only words that trip a person up are *grandmother* and *Spanish*. You will guess at *grandmother* and perhaps say *grandfather* or *grandparents*. But it is a guess. Usually the *Spanish* cannot even be read. Unless you are familiar with horses, Spanish stallion isn't in a your listening vocabulary, and there are not enough clues to guess the word.

Phoneme Segmentation from page 69

Read the words below and count the number of phonemes you hear. Remember, it is not the number of letters in a word, but the number of sounds.

bringing   station   thing
hopeless   institution packing

Answers to segmenting words.

Word	Sounds	Number
bringing	/b/-/r/-/i/-/ng/-/i/-/ng/	6
hopeless	/h/-/o/-/p/-/l/-/e/-/s/	6
thing	/th/-/i/-/ng/	3
station	/s/-/t/-/a/-/sh/-/o/-/n/	6
institution	/i/-/n/-/s/-/t/-/i/-/t/-/oo/-/sh/-/o/-/n/	10
packing	/p/-/a/-/k/-/i/-/ng/	5

Bibliography

Adams, J. M. (1990). Beginning to read: Thinking and learning about print. Cambridge, MA: MIT Press.

Adlof, S., Catts, H., & Weismer, S. (2006, April). Language deficits in poor comprehenders: a case for the simple view of reading. Journal of Speech, Language, and Hearing, 49, 278–293.

Allen, K. A., Newhaus, G. F., & Beckwith, M. C. (2005). Alphabet knowledge: Letter recognition, naming, and sequencing. In Birsh, J. R (Ed.), Multisensory Teaching of Basic Language Skills, Second Edition (83-112). Baltimore, MD: Paul H. Brooke, Publishing Co.

Anbar, A. (1986). Reading acquisition of preschool children without systematic instruction. Early Childhood Research Quarterly I, 69-83.

Anbar, A. (2004). The Secret of Natural Readers. Westport, CT: Praeger Publishers

Anderson, R. C., & Nagy, W. E. (1992, Winter). The vocabulary. conundrum American Educator: The Professional Journal of the American Federation of Teachers, 16(4), 14-18, 44-47.

Ball, E. W., & Blachman, B. A. (1991). Does phoneme awareness training in kindergarten make a difference in early word recognition and developmental spelling? Reading Research Quarterly, 16 (1), 49-66.

Balmuth, M. (1982). The roots of phonics: A historical introduction, Baltimore, MD: Paul H. Brookes Publishing Co., Inc.

Balmuth, M. (2009). The roots of phonics: A historical introduction, Revised Edition, Baltimore, MD: Paul H. Brookes Publishing Co., Inc.

Beck, I. L, McKeown, M. G. & Kucan, L. (2002). Bringing words to life: Robust vocabulary instruction. New York, NY: Guilford Press.

Bodrova, E., & Leong, D. J. (1996). Tools of the mind: A Vygotskian approach to early childhood education. Englewood Cliffs, NJ: Prentice-Hall.

Bradley, L., & Bryant, P. E. (1983). Categorizing sounds and learning to read--a causal connection. Nature, 30, 419-421.

Bradley, L., & Bryant, P. E. (1985). Rhyme and reason in reading and spelling. Ann Arbor: University of Michigan Press.

Bradley, L., & Bryant, P. E. (1991). Phonological skills before and after learning to read. In S. A. Brady & D. P. Shankweiler (Eds.), Phonological processes in literacy: A tribute to Isabelle Y. Liberman. Hillsdale, NJ: Erlbaum.

Brady S. A., & Shankweiler, D. P. (Eds.). (1991). Phonological processes in literacy: A tribute to Isabelle Y. Liberman. Hillsdale, NJ: Erlbaum.

Brown, J. L. (1970, May). You can read faster. Reader's Digest, Pleasantville, NY: The Reader's Digest Association.

Bryant, D. P., Goodwin, M., Bryant, B. R., & Higgins, K. (2003). Vocabulary instruction for students with learning disabilities: A review of research. Learning Disability Quarterly, 26, 117–128.

Burns, M. L. (2012). Modern physics for science and engineering. Physics Curriculum & Instruction, Inc. www.physicscurriculum.com

Calfee, R., & Henry, M. (1996). Strategy and skill in early reading acquisition. In J. Shimron (Ed), Literacy and education: essays in memory of Dina Feitelson (pp. 47-68). Cresskill, NJ: Hampton Press.

Cardoso-Martins. C., Mesquita. T., & Ehri, L. (2011). Letter names and phonological awareness help children to learn letter-sound relations. Journal of Experimental Child Psychology 109 (2011) 25-38.

Catts, H. (April 2009). The narrow view of reading promotes a broad view of comprehension. Language, Speech & Hearing Services in School, 40, 188–193.

Chall, J. S. (1996). Stages of reading development. Forth Worth, TX: Harcourt Brace College Publishers.

Clay, M. M. (1979). Reading: The patterning of complex behavior. Auckland, New Zealand: Heinemann.

Cudd, E. T, & Roberts, L. (1989). Using writing to enhance content area learning in the primary grades. Reading Teacher, 42 (6), 392-404.

Davis, R. D., (2010). The Gift of Dyslexia: Why Some of the Smartest People Can't Read and How They Can Learn. New York, NY: Perigree Books.

de Garcia, L. A. (2018). Bilateral integration. Whole Child Learning Solutions. Retrived from: https://www.wholechildlearningsolutions.com/bilateral-integration.html

Durkin, D. (1966). Children who read early. New York: Teacher's College Press.

Ehri, L. C. (1983). A critique of five studies related to letter-name knowledge and learning to read. In L. M. Gentile, M. L. Kamil, & J. S. Blanchard (Eds.), Reading research revisited (pp. 143–153). Columbus, OH: Merrill.

Ehri, L C. (1991). Development of the ability to read words. In R. Barr, M. L Kamii, P. Mosenthal & P. D. Pearson (eds.). Handbook of Reading Research. New York, NY: Longman. 2, 383 -4 17.

Fernald, G. (1943). Remedial techniques in basic school subjects. New York, NY: McGraw-Hill Book Company, Inc.

Gold, S. (2008). If children came with instruction sheets. Eugene: FernRidge Press.

Good, R. H., & Kaminski, R. A. (Eds.). (2007). Dynamic Indicators of Basic Early Literacy Skills (6th ed.). Eugene, OR: Institute for the Development of Educational Achievement.

Goswami, U. C., & Bryant, P. E. (1990). Phonological skills and learning to read. East Sussex, BN: Lawrence Erlbaum Associates Ltd, Publishers.

Graves, D. H. (1994). A fresh look at writing. Portsmouth, NJ: Heinemann.Hart, B., & Risley, T. R. (1997). Meaningful differences in the everyday experience of young American children. Baltimore, MD: Paul H. Brookes Publishing Co.

Hasbrouck, J. E., & Tindal, G., (1992). Curriculum-based oral reading fluency norms for students in grades 2 through 5. Teaching Exceptional Children, 24, pp. 41-44.

Henderson, E. H. (1992). The interface of lexical competence and knowledge of written words. In S. Templeton & D. R. Bear (Eds.), Development of orthographic knowledge and the foundations of literacy: A memorial Festschrift of Edmunch H. Henderson (pp. 1-3). Hillsdale, NJ: Erlbaum.

Henderson, E. H., & Beers, J. W. (Eds.). (1980). Developmental and cognitive aspects of learning to spell: A reflection of word knowledge. Newark, DE: International Reading Association.

Henderson, L. & Chard, J. (1980). The reader's implicit knowledge of orthographic structure. In U. Frith (Ed.), Cognitive processes in spelling (p. 85-116). New York: Academic Press.

Henry, M. K. (2005). The history and structure of written English. In Birsh, J. R (Ed.), Multisensory Teaching of Basic Language Skills, Second Edition (83-112). Baltimore, MD: Paul H. Brooke, Publishing Co.

Herron, J. (2008, September). Why phonics teaching must change. Educational Leadership. Association for Supervision and Curriculum Development. p. 77 – 81.

Honig, B. (2001). Teaching Our Children to Read. Thousand Oaks, CA: Corwin Press, Inc.

Honigsfeld, A., & Dunn, R. (2009). Learning-style responsive approaches for teaching typically performing and at-risk adolescents. The Clearing House, 82 (5), 220-224.

Hoover, W. A., & Gough, P. B. (1990). The simple view of reading. Reading and Writing: an Interdisciplinary Journal, 2, 126-160. Netherlands: Kluwer Academic Publishers.

Huey, E. B. (1908). The psychology and pedagogy of reading. New York: Macmillan.

Juel, C. (1994a). Learning to read and write in one elementary school. New York, NY: Springer-Verlag.

Juel, C. (1994b). Teaching phonics in the context of the integrated language arts. In L. M. Morrow et al. (Eds.). Integrated Language Arts (pp. 133 - 154). Needham Heights, MA: Allyn and Bacon.

Juel, C., & Roper/Schneider, D. (1985.) The influence of basal readers on first grade reading. Reading Research Quarterly, 18, 134-152.

Keene, E. O. & Zimmerman, S. (1997). Mosaic of thought: teaching comprehension. Reader's Workshop, p. 141'

Kim, Y., Petscher, Y., & Foorman, B. (2010, May). Contributions of phonological awareness and letter-name knowledge to letter-sound acquisition—a cross-classified multilevel model approach. Journal of Educational Psychology, 102 (2), 313-326.

Kinnune, R., & Vauras, M. (1998). Comprehension monitoring in beginning readers. Scientific Studies of Reading, 2(4), 353- 375.

Kuhl P. Williams K, & Lacerda F, (1992). Linguistic experience alters phonetic perception in infants by 6 months of age. Science, 255, 606-608.

Kuhl, P. K., Stevens, E, Hayashi, A. Deguchi,T., Kiritanif, S., & Paul Iverson, P. (2006). Infants show a facilitation effect for native language phonetic perception between 6 and 12 months. Developmental Science, 9 (2), F13-F21.

Learning Stewards (2011). Children of the Code. Retrieved from http://www.childrenofthecode.org/

Liberman, I. Y., Shankweiler, D., Fischer, F. W., & Carter, B. (1974). Explicit syllable and phoneme segmentation in the young child. Journal of Experimental Child Psychology. 18, 201-212.

Liberman, I.Y., Shankweiler, D., & Liberman, A.M. (1989). The Alphabetic principle and learning to read. In Shankweiler and Liberman (Eds.), Phonology and Reading Disability: Solving the Reading Puzzle, University of Michigan Press.

Linksman, R. (2011). The fine line between ADHD and kinesthetic learners. Association for Comprehensive Neurotherapy. Palm Beach, FL: Retrieved from http://www.latitudes.org/articles/learn01.html

McKeown, M. C., Beck, I. L, & Blake, R. (2009). Rethinking reading comprehension instruction: a comparison of instruction for strategies and content approaches. Reading Research Quarterly. 44 (3), 218- 253.

Moats, L. (1998, Spring/Summer). Teaching decoding. American Educator, 42-49, 95-96.

Moats, L. (2004, October). Relevance of neuroscience to effective education for students with reading and other learning disabilities. Journal of Child Neurology, 19(10), 840-845.

Moats (2009). The challenge of learning to read, 2nd ed. Longmont, CO: Sopris West Educational Services.

Montessori, M. (1964). The Montessori method. New York: Schocken Books.

Morais, J. (1991). Constraints on the development of phonemic awareness. In D. Shankweiler (Ed.), Phonological processes in literacy: A tribute to Isabelle Y. Liberman (pp. 5-28). Hillsdale, NJ: Lawrence Erlbaum Associates, Publishers.

Morris, D., & Perney, J. (1984). Developmental spelling as a predictor of first-grade reading. The Elementary School Journal, 84 (4), 441-457.

Moran, C., & Calfee, R. (1993). Comprehending orthography: social construction of letter-sound in monolingual and bilingual programs. Reading and Writing: An Interdisciplinary Journal, 5, 205-225.

Nagy, W. E., & Herman, P. A. (1987). Breadth and depth of vocabulary knowledge: Implications for acquisition and instruction. In M. G. McKeown & M. E. Curtis (Eds.). The nature of vocabulary acquisition (pp. 19–35). Hillsdale, NJ: Erlbaum.

Nagy, W. E, & Anderson, R. C. (1984). How many words are there in printed school English? Reading Research Quarterly, 19(3), 304 -330.

NAEP (2002) NAEP oral reading fluency scale, grade 4: 2002. : U.S. Department of Education, Institute of Education Sciences, National Center for Education Statistics Retrieved from http://nces.ed.gov/nationsreportcard/studies/ors/scale.asp

National Institute of Child Health and Human Development (NICHD), (2000). Report of the national reading panel: an evidence-based assessment of the scientific research literature on reading and its implications for reading instruction. NIH Publication No. 00-4754. Washington, DC: U.S. Government Printing Office. Retrieved from http://www.nichd.nih.gov/publications/nrp/smallbook.cfm

Nichols, J. N. (1980). Using paragraph frames to help remedial high school students with written assignments. Journal of Reading, 24 (3),228-31.

Nist, J. (1966). A structural history of English. New York NY; St. Martin's Press.

Papanicolaou A. C., Simos, P. G,, & Fletcher J. M.(2003). Early development and plasticity of neurophysiological processes involved in reading, in Foorman, B.F. (ed): Preventing and Remediating Reading Difficulties: Bringing Science to Scale. Baltimore, MD, York Press, 2003, p. 3-21.

Quitadamo, I.J. & Kurtz, M.J. (Summer 2007). Learning to improve: using writing to increase critical thinking performance in general education biology. CBE Life Science Education 6(2),140-54.

Read, C. (1975). Children's categorization of speech sounds in English. Urbana, IL: National Council of Teachers of English.

Reading by Touch. (1948, July 12). Time. Retrieved from http://www.time.com/time/magazine/article/0,9171,804743-1,00.html

Shankweiler, D. (1991). The contribution of Isabell Y. Liberman. In D. Shankweiler (Ed.), Phonological processes in literacy: A tribute to Isabelle Y. Liberman (pp. xiii-xvii). Hillsdale, NJ: Lawrence Erlbaum Associates, Publishers.

Shaywitz, S. (November 1996). 10 years of brain imaging research shows the brain reads sound by sound. Scientific American, pp. 98-104. Retrieved from http://kidsadhd.com/learning/brain.shtml

Shaywitz, B. A., Shaywitz, S. E., Pugh, K. R., Mencl, W. E., Fulbright, R.K., Skudlarski, P., & Gore, J. C. (2002). Disruption of posterior brain systems for reading in children with developmental dyslexia. Society of Biological Psychiatry.

Shaywitz, S (2003). Overcoming Dyslexia. New York, NY: Alfred A. Knopf, a division of Random House, Inc.

Shaywitz, B. A., Shaywitz, S. E., Blachman, B. A., Pugh, K. R. Fulbright, R. K., Skudlarski, P. & Goret, J. C. (May 2004). Development of left occipitotemporal systems for skilled reading in children after a phonologically based intervention. Biological psychiatry 255, p. 926-933. Found online at http://www.haskins.yale.edu/papers/intervention_biol_psych_200.pdf

Simos, P.G., Fletcher, J. M., Bergman, E., Breier, J. I., Foorman, B. R., Castillo, E. M., & Papanicolaou, A. C. (April 2002). Dyslexia-specific brain activation profile becomes normal following successful remedial training. Neurology, 58.

Spaulding, R.& North, M (2003). Writing road to reading. New York, NY: Harper Collins Publishers, Inc.

Sporleder, R. (1995). Early spontaneous readers. Unpublished manuscript.

Sporleder, R. L. (1998, April). A comparison of three approaches to literacy acquisition: Traditional phonics, whole language, and spelling before reading. Doctoral dissertation Montana State University, Bozeman, Montana.

Sporleder, R. L. (2012). Roxie Reading C. Marion, IN: Teaching Basics.

Stuart, M., & Coltheart, M. (1989). Does reading develop in a sequence of stages? Cognition, 30, 139-181.The Melisa Institute for Violence Prevention and Treatment, (n.d.).Vocabulary development. Retrieved from http://www.teachsafeschools.org/vocabulary_nurtur.html

Treiman, R., Tincoff, R., & Rodriguez, K.(1998, December). The foundations of literacy: learning the sounds of letters. Child Development, 69 (6), 1524-1540.

Uhry, J. K. (2005). Phonemic awareness and reading: research, activities, and instructional materials. In Birsh, J. R (Ed.), Multisensory Teaching of Basic Language Skills, Second Edition (83-112). Baltimore, MD: Paul H. Brooke, Publishing Co.

Venezky, R. L. (1970). The structure of English orthography. The Hague, Paris: Mouton.

Wagner, R. K., & Torgesen, J. K. (1987). The nature of phonological processing and its causal role in the acquisition of reading skills. Psychological Bulletin, 101 (2), 192-212.

White, S. (1995, August). Listening to children read aloud: oral fluency. Washington, DC: National Center for Education Statistics. Retrieved from http://nces.ed.gov/pubs95/web/95762.asp

Yeh, S.S. & Connell, D. B (2008). Effects of rhyming, vocabulary and phonemic awareness instruction on phonemic awareness. Journal of Research in Reading, 31(2), 243-256.

Index

A

Abraham Lincoln 139
Accent 41, 82, 87, 126, 174
Acting out the sound 75-76, 201, 207
Actions for the sounds 207-208, 210, 212, 214
ADD 10, 16
Adding suffixes 85, 175, 199, 218
ADHD 10, 16, 24, 228
Affixes See Prefixes. See Suffixes.
Alphabet 41, 43, 48-49, 64, 69-73, 76-77, 80-82, 94, 164, 166, 168-169, 175, 178, 198, 225
Alphabetic principle 166, 170, 228
Amount of time reading 133, 134
Anticipate and prevent errors 25, 96
Approximation of sounds 82
Art and kinesthetic learners 21
Ask questions 25-26, 96-97, 131, 144-145, 148
Assessing foundational skills 164, 166, 168, 170, 172, 174, 176, 178, 180, 182, 184, 186, 188
Assessments four basic 187
Attention span 27, 194
Athletics and kinesthetic learners 21
Auditory learner 18-19, 21, 28
Auditory skill, phonemic awareness 59

B

Background knowledge 16, 138-140, 142-143
Base reading speed 123
Base word 97-98, 107, 199
Beyond the alphabet 80, 82, 168
Big picture 23, 33, 38, 84
Blending 65, 104-105
Brain 20, 34, 40-48, 50, 52-53, 60, 67, 70-71, 73-75, 80, 92-94, 97, 102, 104, 106, 112, 114, 136, 138, 164, 198, 201, 230
  Broca's area 41
  How the brain can change 47
  How the brain reads 44
  Language centers 40-41, 44-48, 53, 112, 138
  Left brain 45-48, 53, 102, 136, 138
  Letter center 40-41, 43, 60, 70-71
  Occipital-temporal 41
  Parieto-temporal 41
  Right side 43, 48, 67, 136
  Sally Shaywitz 40, 43, 48
  Speech sound center 40-41, 43, 48, 60, 70-71
  Word center 40-41, 43, 70, 97, 106, 112, 114, 136, 138, 166
Brain scans of the brain 40, 43, 48
Breaking a word apart 108
Broca's area 41
Building words 91-92, 94, 96, 98, 100, 110

C

Capital letters 74, 152
Cause and effect paragraph 157, 160
Challenge words 108, 110, 128, 200
Chip game 61, 65, 67, 179, 188, 199, 201
Choral reading 117
Chunking words 107, 115-116
Classroom dilemma 135
Clock letters 79
Computers 21, 32
Concept map 23
Confusing graphemes 81
Confusing letters 78
Context to "guess" words 128
Creative projects 33, 38
Cross lateral exercise 80, 201
C say /s/ 84, 87-88, 90, 176, 216, 218

D

Davis R. D. 22
Decodable texts 129-130
Decoding 16, 93, 101-108, 110, 112, 114-115, 117, 129, 136, 138, 166, 168, 185, 188, 195, 199-201, 228
  Simple words 84, 102, 106, 166, 186
  Multisyllable words 107-108, 141, 166, 185, 186, 199, 200
  Decoding problems 103-105, 109, 110
Demonstrations and experiments 20, 32, 38

Developmental spelling test 167, 170-172, 175-176, 188, 198
_dge 49, 64, 81, 88, 90, 187, 205, 217
Diagrams 20, 33, 38
Direct perception reading 121
Disabilities 15, 21, 52, 190, 195, 226, 228
Dramatic reading 116
Dramatization 32
Drawings 33
Dyslexia 16, 21-22, 40, 43, 226, 230

E

Echo reading 116
English language learners 190
Errorless learning 25, 28, 37, 42, 50, 52, 66, 70, 80, 92, 94, 102, 112, 128, 151, 164, 198
Experiments 20, 32, 38
Eye span 113, 122
Eye–voice span 114

F

Fair readers 177
Feedback 25-26, 28, 61, 63, 66, 80, 151, 188, 198
Eernald, Grace 34
Field trips 33, 38, 143
Fine muscles 19, 27-28
Flashcards 31
Fluency 6-7, 44, 111-118, 131-132, 138, 165-168, 170, 177, 185-188, 227, 229, 231
Fluency also See Saccade.
Fluency problem 114-115
Four basic assessments 167
Fourth grade crash 44
Framework for teaching reading 3, 165-167
Frustration reading level 130-131

G

Games 28, 32-33, 38, 63, 65, 77-78, 81, 128, 165, 177, 188, 192, 198-199
Good readers 40-41, 52, 93, 112, 133, 139, 177
Grace Fernald 34
Grammar and sentence structure 158
"graph" definition 70

Graphemes. See Spellings of the Sounds.
Graphic organizers 23, 33, 38, 156

H

Habit of rereading 121, 124, 125
Hearing impaired 191
Hearing sounds in spoken words 51-52, 54, 56, 58
Hindrances to silent reading speed 121, 122
Hold a pencil properly 78
Horizontal line letters 80
Horse 44, 222
How the brain can change 47, 48
How we learn 18
How we read 113, 123

I

Identifying fluency problem 114, 115
Impact on parents 10
Impact on society 11
Impact on teachers 10
Incomplete sentence 152
Independent reading level 130-131
Individual sounds of speech. See Phonemes.
Inferences 144, 150
Informal reading analysis 167, 185, 187-188
Instant retrieval of words 43, 45, 106, 112
Instant word recognition 106
Instructional level 26, 36, 132-136, 138, 143, 185, 188, 200
Instructional reading level 130, 132, 185
Intellectual disability 195
ipad 30, 94
Isolated texts 143

J

Just right book 131, 132, 134

K

K at the beginning of words 87, 90
Kinesthetic decoding 104, 105, 201
Kinesthetic learners 18-24, 28, 30, 32-33, 42, 60, 61, 78, 228
Knowledge base 11, 13, 45, 132, 136, 139-140, 142-144

L

Language centers 40-41, 44-48, 53, 112, 138
Large muscles 18-20, 24, 28, 32, 38, 77, 80, 94,
Learning disabilities 21, 190, 226, 228
Learning styles. 30, 59, 61
Left side of the brain 20, 40, 43, 48
Letter recognition test 167, 169
Letter tiles 31, 77, 164
Limit "teacher talk 94
Line letters 79
Linksman, Ricki 24
Listening vocabulary 109, 129, 141-142, 159, 222
Long vowels 63, 85, 166, 184, 204
Long vowel sounds 49, 63, 72
Louisa Moats 93

M

Magic "e" 85
Manipulate cards 61
Manipulate sounds 54-55, 68, 167, 168, 181,
"marker ready" words 88, 89, 219
Markers 30, 83-90, 110, 186-187, 216
Maximum reading growth 131-132
Mechanics and kinesthetic learners 21
Moats, Louisa 93
Moving the lips 120-122, 124
Music and kinesthetic learner 21

N

Need to know why 20, 38
Neuroimaging 40
Neuroscientists 40, 42, 50
Non-reading activities 128

O

Oral reading fluency rubric 186
Oral reading speed 112
Oral sentence 152-153

P

Paragraph 19, 131, 133, 150-151, 154-158, 160-162, 229
Paragraph frame 155, 158, 161
Paragraph types 158
Parietal-temporal 41

Pencil always stays in the hand 151, 155, 157, 162
Phoneme-based phonics 4
Phoneme manipulation Test 167, 178, 188
Phonemes See Speech Sounds.
Phoneme segmentation test 167, 178-180
Phonemic awareness 3, 28, 53-54, 58-62, 64-68, 78, 81, 92, 102, 104-105, 114-115, 128, 138, 164-168, 170-172, 175, 177-178, 190, 192, 194-195, 198-199, 220, 229-231
Phonemic awareness assessments 67-68, 178
Phonics 52, 85, 93, 177, 225, 227, 230
"phono" definition 52
Pictures and drawings 33
Picture thinker 21-22
Poor readers 10, 16, 18, 20, 41, 43, 45-47, 49, 63, 65-66, 78, 80-81, 114, 120, 128, 136, 138, 152, 170, 177
  What they do not know 49-50
  What they usually know 48-49—
Powerful questions 138, 144-147
Prefixes 42, 50, 52, 70, 76, 92, 97-99, 102, 106, 109-110, 112, 164, 166-168, 170, 176, 187, 198-199, 217
Pre-teaching 37
Prevent errors 25, 26, 96
Prior knowledge 138, 140
Problem solving 32-33
Pronouncing sounds 57
Pronunciation issues in decoding 109
Proofread 151

Q

Questions 25-26, 144-147, 150, 153-155, 162, 168, 174, 181
Question and sentence answer 150, 151, 154-155, 162

R

R. Davis 22
Read aloud 112, 114, 117, 142, 165, 231
Read at the right level 128, 130, 132, 134, 136
Read challenge words 128, 200

Reading comprehension 10, 13, 16, 44, 47, 93, 114, 117, 121, 124-125, 132, 135-136, 138-140, 142-144, 148, 155, 158-159, 165, 170, 177, 200, 226, 228
Reading level 12-13, 49, 130-132, 134-135, 167, 170, 185, 200
Reading log 134
Reading time 26, 121, 125, 134, 136
Reading word by word 121-122
Read 30 minutes a day 134, 136, 157, 200
Read the tops of words 126
Read the words they have spelled 128
Read word by word 43, 113, 115, 120-121
Record sheet for reading speed 123, 124
Rereading 121, 124
Rereading or looking back 121
Researchers 41-42, 50, 60, 74, 78, 121, 195
Resource room 21, 34-36, 77
Reteaching 37
Ricki Linksman 24
Right content 11-12, 14, 40, 42, 44, 46-48, 50, 52, 93, 134-135, 164, 168, 190-191, 195, 198, 202
Right instruction 11-12, 42, 47, 50, 52, 70, 92-93, 102, 112, 134-135, 164, 190-191, 193, 195, 198, 202
Right sequence 11-12, 14, 42, 47, 50, 52, 93, 134-135, 190-191, 195, 198, 202
Rule of v 89, 216, 217
Rules of syllabication 106

S

Saccade 113
Sally Shaywitz 40, 43, 48
School assignments 119
Scientific research 11, 15, 93, 229
Self-check list 151, 153, 157
Sense of achievement 24-26, 36, 128
Sensory learning styles 18, 28, 30, 60-61
Sentence 31, 34-36, 46, 113, 115-116, 131, 133, 150-158, 160-162, 167, 170, 200
Sentence frame 153-156, 160
Sentence, oral 152, 153

Short vowel sounds 49, 55, 63, 72, 178, 198
Sight words 93, 112
Silent "e" 85
Silent reading speed 119, 121-122, 124, 126
Simple (small) words 84, 102, 106, 166
Skinny L 86
Slant line letters 79
Slash marks 53, 109
Small group 32, 37-38, 63, 68, 117, 134, 177-178
Sound card assessment 167, 178, 182
Sound cards 60-61, 63, 183-184, 188, 190
Sounding out a word 102
Special education 11, 13, 80, 110
Special situations 189-190, 192, 194, 196
Speech sound center 40-41, 43, 48, 60, 70-71
Speech sounds 41-42, 50, 52-53, 70, 72, 75, 78, 82, 92-93, 97, 102, 112, 164, 172, 190, 198, 203-204, 206, 229
Speed readers 121, 126
Spell before reading 92, 93
Spelling lists 159, 171
Spellings of /k 87
Spellings of phonemes 70, 71, 73, 75, 77, 80. 81, 82, 90. 92, 95, 97, 102,105, 106,108, 128, 129, 133, 194, 195, 202-206
Start with print 92, 93
Stopping the marker 85, 88
Story board 21
Strategies for kinesthetic learners 29-30, 32, 34, 36, 38
Struggling readers. see Poor Readers.
Students
    April 2nd grade 13, 190
    Ben 3rd grade crashed at 5th 44
    Brittany 3rd grade vision issue 194, 195
    Daniel 2nd grade vision issue 195
    Drew 3rd grade resource room 134-136, 80, 154
    Jakob 7th grade special ed 13, 14, 190
    Jared 11th grade 13, 14, 20
    Joel 1st grade decoding issue 104
    John 11th grade 14, 26

Kevin 11th grade writing disabled 47
Kyle 1st grade learns letters 77, 78
Manuel 2nd- 4th grade 16
Mia 1st grade alphabet issue 77
Owen 5th grade speech impediment 126
Sean 6th grade at primer level 13, 26
Sheri 1st grade hearing impairment 192
Tanya 7th grade 135
Temica 2nd grade special ed 76

Subvocalizing 124
Suffixes 42, 50, 52, 56, 70, 76, 85-86, 88, 90, 92, 97-99, 102, 106-107, 109-110, 112, 141, 164, 166-168, 170, 175-176, 187, 198-199, 216, 218
Supporting detail 156

T

Tactile learner 18-21, 28
Text structure 158
The fine line between ADHD and 24
The gift of dyslexia 22
The Horse 45-46, 222
The "Real Rules" of English 2, 4, 8, 167, 175, 199, 201, 215-216, 218, 220
Think-read method of reading 120, 121
Think while reading 167
Three dimensional thinking 22-23, 78
Timed reading activities 122-126
Timeline 23
Topic sentence 156-157, 160
Tracing the letters 80
Traditional reading instruction
Traditional sequence 73, 74
Two frogs 146
Two vowels make separate sounds 110
Types of silent reading 120-121

U

Understand the meaning 43, 100, 141
Units of instruction 143
Unstressed syllables 85, 87, 110, 217

V

Venn diagram 23
Verbal clues 78
Very poor readers 177
Vision impairments 105, 192-193

Visualization 140
Visual learner 18-21, 28
Vocabulary 7, 13, 16, 32, 45-47, 66, 98, 108-109, 129, 132, 136, 140-143, 159, 177-178, 222, 225-226, 229-231
Vocabulary stalls 132, 141
Vocalizing method of reading 120
Voiced and unvoiced pairs 55-58, 62, 176-177, 220
Voicing punctuation 116
Vowel long 84-88, 90, 186, 218

W

What you need to know 42, 71, 99, 168
What students need 24
Whiteboards 19, 20, 30, 61, 80, 94, 100, 154, 192, 199, 200-201
Woodcock Reading Mastery Test 11, 13, 47, 126, 135, 185
Word building 3, 94, 96, 99, 128, 152, 198-199
Word center 40-41, 43, 70, 97, 106, 112, 114, 136, 138, 166
Words per minute 120-121, 123-124, 126
Working memory 44, 138
Writing 10, 16, 18, 19, 20, 25-28, 30, 36, 38, 47, 77-80, 91, 94, 98, 141, 144-145, 149-162, 164-165, 172, 176, 178, 200-201, 226-227, 229-230
Writing disabled 10, 16, 47, 165
Writing letters 77-78, 164

Y

Young children 71, 94, 142

www.ingramcontent.com/pod-product-compliance
Lightning Source LLC
Chambersburg PA
CBHW051403070526
44584CB00023B/3274